THE ELEMENTS OF HU

CW00358291

Nevill Drury was born in England in
life in Australia. An internationally
of holistic health and the esoteric trad
interest in the Human Potential Movem................ ....
states of consciousness. He holds a Master's degree in anthropology
and is editor of *Nature & Health* journal.

THE ELEMENTS OF

HUMAN POTENTIAL

Nevill Drury

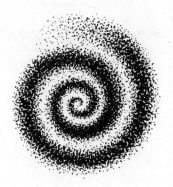

ELEMENT BOOKS

© Nevill and Susan Drury Publishing Pty Ltd 1989

First published in 1989 by
Element Books Limited
Longmead, Shaftesbury, Dorset

Designed by Jenny Liddle
Cover design by Max Fairbrother

Typeset in 9/11 Melior by Selectmove Ltd, London
Printed and bound in Great Britain by Billings
Hylton Road, Worcester

British Library Cataloguing in Publication Data
Drury, Nevill 1947–
The elements of human potential
1. Self-realisation
I. Title
158'.1

ISBN 1-85230-086-8

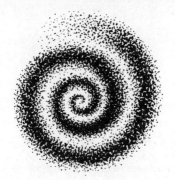

CONTENTS

We are a more extraordinary animal than we think,
but also a more dangerous one;
we are closer to destruction
and to transcendence, than we know,
in a race with the different pieces of ourselves.

Robert E. Ornstein, *Multimind*

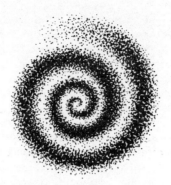

INTRODUCTION

Since the early 1970s I have been involved in writing primarily on the Western esoteric traditions, but it soon became apparent to me that what really interested me was *consciousness* itself. I became increasingly preoccupied with ways of exploring the visionary areas of the mind – through art, ambient music, visualisation and, more recently, shamanic drum-beat meditation. I found myself researching the mythic areas of contemporary art, especially the surrealism and visionary imagery of such masters as Max Ernst, Magritte, Austin Spare and Ernst Fuchs, and I was intrigued by the spiritual quest of Carl Jung, as described in his inspiring *Memories, Dreams, Reflections*. Also I read widely in the literature of shamanism and psychedelic research to learn more of the human potentials revealed through altered states of consciousness, especially in relation to the spiritual archetypes of the mind. All of this – as I realise now – was leading me towards the Human Potential Movement.

In 1980 I was privileged to be involved as a guest lecturer at the International Transpersonal Conference which was being held for the first time in Australia at Phillip Island, a short drive from Melbourne. This gave me the opportunity to meet several of the leading figures from the Human Potential Movement for the first time, including Michael Harner, Stanislav Grof, Ralph Metzner and James Fadiman. It was an inspiring conference, which changed my orientation from what I now perceive as the relative confines of the Western occult traditions, towards a much broader-based concern with mythic areas of consciousness. The shamanic drum-beat technique I learned from Michael Harner, for example, leads one directly into regions of the mind which become for the voyager a type of Dreamtime. Here mythic images rise up from the depths of the psyche with remarkable and awe-inspiring clarity.

Around this time, too, I was becoming interested in the paradigm of holistic health and in 1983 was appointed editor of *Nature & Health*, an internationally oriented health journal. I still edit this journal, and believe it has provided me with many opportunities to explore the broad directions of the Human Potential Movement first-hand. We have featured in our pages interviews with many of the figures who have helped shape the New Consciousness and there have been many lectures and workshops to attend.

The rise of the holistic health paradigm and the emergence of Transpersonal psychology as the 'fourth force' following Psycho-analysis, Behaviourism and Humanistic psychology, has owed much to the influence of the Esalen Institute in California – a centre I was able to visit in 1979 and again in 1984. So many of the people described in these pages are people whom I have met and whose opinions I value personally.

It seems to me that the rise of the Human Potential Movement as a whole is a very exciting development indeed: what could be more relevant or absorbing than the study of human consciousness itself? It also leads us to ask questions about our perceptions, values and religious beliefs – in particular, whether what we believe is reflected in the evidence emerging in the new paradigms of consciousness research. The Human Potential Movement and its popular offshoot, the New Age, help focus our attention on these important issues.

The reader will notice that I have not attempted to downplay the role of psychedelics in the development of the Human Potential Movement. Many of the leading figures in the New Counsciousness, including Doctors Stanislav Grof, John Lilly, Jean Houston and Ralph Metzner, have all been previously involved in scientific psychedelic research and continue to value the insights it provided into the nature of human consciousness. Indeed, the holistic health paradigm began to emerge in the early 1970s in part as a non-drug response to the psychedelic exploration undertaken in the 1960s.

I hasten to emphasise that this book is very much an introductory overview of the themes in the Human Potential Movement which I feel are significant, and this is in no way a definitive history: that still remains to be written. Because of considerations of length, many individual therapies and specialist areas of research have not been described, and readers are urged to use this book to initiate further inquiry in directions of personal interest. What I have tried to do here is to convey my feeling that the Human Potential Movement is a very important force in the shaping of contemporary social and religious awareness, for its focuses on a task we all share – to explore more fully our shared potentials in body, mind and spirit. If we all participate in that, then the world can only become a better place to live in.

Nevill Drury
Sydney, 1989

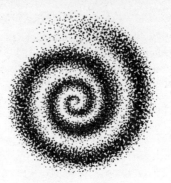

1 · BRAIN,
MIND AND
CONSCIOUSNESS

By definition psychology ought to be the study of the *psyche* – mind, consciousness or 'soul'. But for several decades psychology has wrestled with the need to become truly scientific – to measure, to validate, to objectify. As a consequence it has tended to turn away from the intangibles of human experience like emotions, feelings, intuitions and aesthetic values and has concentrated instead on the more specific aspects of behaviour.

Leading the original charge towards objectivity was John B. Watson, the first acknowledged psychological behaviourist. Watson denied the existence of consciousness, arguing that all learning was a response to the environment, that despite genetic variables human actions could be readily conditioned and modified. Watson defined psychology as follows:

> Psychology as the behaviourist views it is a purely objective branch of natural science. Its theoretical goal is the prediction and control of behaviour. Introspection forms no essential part of its methods. . . . The behaviourist, in his efforts to get a unitary scheme of animal response, recognises no dividing line between man and brute.[1]

The behaviourist tradition was consolidated by Ivan Pavlov's work on controlling behaviour and by B.F. Skinner's influential concepts relating to conditioning and reinforcement as part of learning theory. Skinner rejected the concept of the 'personality' arguing that the latter was simply a collection of behaviour patterns, as were the emotions and intellect. Likewise, for Skinner the notion of the 'self' was not essential in analysing behaviour and any idea of self-knowledge was a convenient fiction. 'There is no place in the scientific position', he wrote in 1974, 'for a self as a true originator or initiator of action.'[2]

However, with the development of phenomenology, transpersonal research and the experiential psychotherapies, Skinner's approach has begun to look less and less complete. The Human Potential Movement – which can be seen in part as a response against the limitations of behaviourism – consists substantially of people intent on uncovering the inner motivating forces that reflect and influence behaviour: habitual patterns, fears, intuitions, repressions – and how these interactions work. Personal growth is very much about understanding inner states of being as well as modifying outer forms of behaviour.

We are led, then, to ask what it is that makes us truly human and distinguishes us from other animal species. What is it that helps us to be aware that we are aware – the hallmark of each human as a thinking being? A good starting point in this quest for understanding our 'human-ness' is the human brain itself.

INSIDE THE BRAIN

In purely physical terms the brain is one of the heaviest organs in the body, weighing approximately 1.4 kilograms, and is not unlike a large walnut in appearance.

As you look down upon the brain, it divides neatly into two halves along a mid-line, each half approximately a mirror image of the other. The dominant part of the brain, the cerebrum, is sheathed on its outer surface by the cortex – a wrinkled and fissured layer of grey matter some 3–4 mm thick. Underlying the cortex are the two cerebral hemispheres of the brain, left and right, which have become increasingly important in the fundamental issue of understanding consciousness.

Connecting the two hemispheres is a large bundle of fibres known as the corpus callosum. In normal brain function the corpus callosum allows for integrated mental and physical performance so that the left side of the body is mainly controlled by the right side of the cortex and the right side of the body by the left side of the cortex. However, if the corpus callosum is split surgically the two sides of the brain tend to operate independently.

Beneath the two brain hemispheres is a smaller organ called the cerebellum, which is approximately the size of a clenched fist. It too has a cortex and is bilaterally symmetrical. Its main function seems to be to monitor the fine muscular movements required for co-ordination and purposeful action.

If one were to consider the cerebrum and cerebellum like fruits on a tree, they are indeed connected to a stalk known as the brain stem. Consisting mostly of white matter, this tube is a continuation of the spinal cord, and, together the spinal cord and the brain constitute the central nervous system. The brain stem thickens within the skull cavity and merges into a number of other structures. In this region we find the pineal gland – which Descartes considered to be the seat of the soul – and the pituitary gland which produces hormones affecting physical activities like growth and sexual development.

One of the most intriguing aspects of the brain is the way it seems to have evolved in specific stages over a period of more than 500 million years. It is almost as if one layer has been overlaid on top of another, each part of the brain providing different faculties appropriate to the era in which they developed.

There appear to be three distinct evolutionary phases in the development of the human brain.[3] The earliest stage is represented by the 'reptilean' brain which is located near the top of the brain stem – this is found also in turtles, alligators and lizards and evolved to its present state around 500 million years ago. This part of our brain provides our sense of general alertness but none of the faculties we would associate with the 'higher mind'.

Then there is the 'old mammalian' brain associated with the so-called limbic system, which we share with lower mammals like rats, rabbits, kangaroos and horses. In broad terms it seems to provide the faculties which were required as animals switched from dwelling in the sea to living on the land, and developed to its present stage approximately 200 million years ago. The old mammalian brain provides the basic emotions and sensory responses like hunger, thirst, pain and shock. It also registers responses like the need to act as an aggressor or protector.

Finally, the most recent brain to evolve is the 'new mammalian' brain, or neocortex, which is highly developed in primates – especially *Homo Sapiens*. The neocortex, which includes all of the cortex except the olfactory portions and the so-called hippocampal and piriform areas, has been described as a quilt covering the rest of the brain. It began to grow around half a million years ago, in the second half of the Pleistocene Age. Clearly more efficient in learning new ways to adapt, this 'higher brain' deals more with voluntary movements, while the earlier stages of the brain are linked more to involuntary responses. It is the neocortex which provides the clearest indicator of man's innate potential.

THE TWO HEMISPHERES OF THE BRAIN

The pioneering neurophysiologists of the late nineteenth century were inclined to regard the brain as an homogenous mass, with any part of the brain having a comparatively equal role in any action. However, in more recent times, following on from Roger Sperry's important work dealing with the output systems of the brain, Robert Ornstein, David Galin and other researchers have developed the distinction between the two brain hemispheres which has been so influential in New Age thought.

In broad terms, the two hemispheres of the brain seem to special-ise in different cognitive styles – the left being associated with analytical and logical thought and communication based on words and mathematical concepts, the right with 'holistic' thought, gestalts, artistic pursuits and spatial relationships. These hemis-pheres communicate with each other via the corpus callosum although they seem to act semi-independently.

It is a commonplace generalisation among many New Age devotees that in modern Western society, which is dominated by scientific and technological thinking, we have developed our left brain at the expense of the right. The criticism is that we rely too much on linear thought, on processing information sequentially, and not enough on intuition. Expressed more evocatively, it is said that in the West we operate too much through our heads and not enough through our hearts.

As with all things, however, it is probably the sensitive blend-ing of the two modes, the balance of the middle way, which is the most appropriate. As Robert Ornstein notes in his classical work *The Psychology of Consciousness*, 'It is the polarity and the integration of these two modes of consciousness, the complementary workings of the intellect and the intuitive, which underlie our highest achievements.'[4]

David Galin also confirms this view, 'The analytic and holistic modes are complementary; each provides a dimension which the other lacks. Artists, scientists, mathematicians writing about their own creativity, all report that their work is based on a smooth integration of both modes.'[5]

These two modes may be summarised as follows:

LEFT HEMISPHERE: Verbal, analytic, reductive-into parts; sequential, rational, time-oriented and discontinuous.

RIGHT HEMISPHERE: Non-verbal, holistic, synthetic, visuo-spatial, intuitive, timeless and diffuse.

To some extent enthusiasts of the New Age have become fixated on the distinction between the left and right hemispheres, even though its principal proponent, Robert Ornstein, has now expanded this model. In his lucid and important book *Multimind*, published in 1986, Ornstein outlined his new view – more akin to the evolutionary levels of brain development discussed earlier – that in fact man has several minds: a type of multi-level brain 'built in different eras for different priorities'. According to Ornstein, we have minds for alertness, for emotions, for danger, for comparing sensory information, for avoiding scarcity. As Ornstein notes:

> The human brain is in part archaic: its design is based on the ground plan and the neural mechanisms of primates and, before that, other mammals and, even before that, vertebrates. For example, the structure of the cod-fish's brain, developed millennia ago and unchanged since, contains many of the basic elements of the human brain. The cod-fish even possesses a cerebral cortex (although it is small), a pituitary gland for controlling hormone production, and a cerebellum. In turn, vertebrates like cod-fish accepted many of their neural circuits and routines from much earlier and much simpler multi-celled creatures. . . .
>
> The basic mechanisms of neural action and neurotransmission are identical in all mammals. We are so similar to other animals that many different ones can serve as laboratory models for the human brain. The crawfish can be used as a model of neurotransmission, the pig has a similar capacity for learning, and even complex visual processes can be studied using the cat or the rhesus monkey's occipital cortex.[6]

Ornstein's new emphasis in evaluating the nature of human consciousness is based on the fact that the world is apparently perceived the way it is because humans have *evolved* to evaluate it in that manner. 'All human beings are similarly evolved to select common aspects of the physical surroundings: we possess eyes that receive radiant electromagnetic energy, ears that pick up the mechanical vibrations of the air, a nose that contains receptors for gaseous molecules, specialised touch sensors, and a complex of cells on the tongue shaped to respond to the molecules in food.'[7]

8

As a consequence, Ornstein has now moved beyond his earlier model of the two hemispheres, which essentially divided the mind into rational and intuitive, to a 'multimind' view which proposes that the brain has different 'talent patches' which are adapted specifically to different types of evolutionary functioning and survival. Man's ability to plan, infer, make decisions, produce schemes and so on has probably developed only during the past four million years, associated with the period of rapid cortical growth. Ornstein's new model of the mind is hierarchical. 'We all have data-processing modules specific to each sense, that makes sense of our environment and provides basic information', says Ornstein, 'but we do not have access to all of our talents at once'. Our talents tend to be independent of one another and our mind is therefore best seen as a 'coalition of competing entities'. Later he elaborates this point: '. . .the mind is a kind of bastard hybrid system; a collage comprising many fixed and innate routines, all of which serve the mental operating policies that stretch over millions of years, millions of organisms and millions of situations'.[8]

Examples of talents that humans can draw upon are: activating; informing; smelling; feeling; healing; moving; locating and identifying; calculating; talking; knowing; governing. What we call 'intelligence' is the appropriate blending of these talents in different situations, although the central focus of the mental system's operation is *consciousness*. Yet it is a consciousness which is continually changing, ever adapting to our multiple needs. This has led Ornstein to his multimind framework. This is not to say that we are all schizophrenics – the thoughts of schizophrenics slide from one portion of the mind to another – but we all have many different selves residing within, each pertinent to the different situations which arise in our lives.

PERCEPTION, 'REALITY' AND THE HOLOGRAPHIC MODEL OF CONSCIOUSNESS

Quite aside from the different 'selves' that respond to the outside world there is also the issue of whether what we perceive is to any extent 'real'. Clearly our perceptions involve a dramatic filtering process. For example, the eye transmits less than one trillionth of the information reaching its surface so there is a massive difference between the available sensory data impinging on the eyeball and what the brain subsequently constructs as 'reality'. Our senses clearly operate within a given spectrum and we see the way we do, and agree on what many psychologists now refer to as the 'consensus reality' substantially because, as human beings, we have all evolved with comparable faculties. Again, quoting Ornstein:

> Personal consciousness is outward oriented (and) seems to have evolved for the primary purpose of ensuring individual biological survival. . . . We first select the sensory modalities of personal consciousness from the mass of information reaching us. This is done by a multi-level process of filtration, for the most part sorting out survival-related stimuli. We are then able to *construct* a stable consciousness from the filtered input.[9]

This selectivity of perception, the filtering of data to produce a modified 'reality', has also intrigued Yale neurosurgeon Karl Pribram. According to Pribram we use our mental equipment to 'tune in' to a specific reality, 'It is possible to think of the brain cortex as being like a piano sounding board, where each cell, when stimulated, resonates maximally to a particular frequency with its broad band tuning at approximately one octave. The only difference is that in vision the frequencies are spatial.'[10]

Pribram is also a leading advocate of a viewpoint that has potentially far-reaching implications and which has had a major impact already on the Human Potential Movement: this is the view that in many ways the brain resembles a hologram.

Pribram was fascinated by the fact that many stroke and head-injury victims did not lose specific memory traces and that memory seemed to be distributed across the brain as a whole, even when large parts of the brain were missing. In the mid-1960s Pribram proposed the Holographic Hypothesis of Brain Function in which he suggested that holography might provide a useful way of looking at brain physiology.

A hologram is a type of three-dimensional lens-less photograph. The technique of holography was developed by Dennis Gabor, who was awarded the Nobel Prize for it in 1971. A hologram is created photographically when a beam of light that has encountered an object crosses, and thus interferes with, another beam of light that has not encountered that object. The hologram produces a three-dimensional record of the interference pattern, while a normal photograph is only a two-dimensional image of an object seen from a single perspective.

In his experimental work Pribram undertook extensive tests on the brains of monkeys, using implanted electrodes, and these tests suggested that visual information is radically modified prior to reaching the visual cortex. It seemed to him that incoming information 'collided' as it were, with stored memories and expectations – producing an 'interference pattern' comparable to that found in a hologram. Also of interest to Pribram was the fact that a small fragment of a hologram retains all the characteristics of the whole image. In the same way, any given section of the brain seems to have access to the total content of memory.

Pribram also did an experiment utilising 'white noise' on television, this 'noise', or system of dots, containing 'all possible patterns'. Pribram was interested to see whether brain cells could respond to the field of dots and derive order from a state of apparent chaos. He discovered that the brain cells could indeed pick up patterns in the white noise, and this led him to conclude:

> We are always constructing our own reality out of a great deal of what ordinarily seems like noise. But it is a structured noise: we have ears like radio tuners and eyes like television tuners that pick out particular programs. With other tuners we could be listening to other programs.[11]

Elsewhere Pribram develops this point further, comparing the holographic wave interference patterns, or 'ripples', with what happens in the brain:

> Ripples are vibrations, waves, and the evidence is that individual cells in the brain cortex encode the frequency of waves within a certain band width. Just as the strings of a musical instrument resonate to a specific range of frequency, so do the cells of the brain cortex.[12]

At this point we should also refer to the philosophical theories of the distinguished physicist David Bohm which have influenced, and complement, Karl Pribram's concept of holographic brain function.

Bohm is an American-born Emeritus Professor at the University of London who formerly worked with Einstein and is the author of standard works on relativity and quantum mechanics. Like Pribram, Bohm is concerned that restricted modes of perception have limited our scientific understanding.

Bohm's work in quantum physics has led him to the view that the universe at its most fundamental level is characterised by 'unbroken wholeness', or, in his own words, 'that-which-is'. For him, all things, including space, time and matter, are aspects of this unbroken wholeness, or totality of existence, which he calls the 'enfolded' or 'implicate' order. However, our science, influenced by the Cartesian philosophy, only perceives separate parts of the Universe, which Bohm calls the 'unfolded' or 'explicate' order. Using the reductionist methods of modern science prevents us from grasping that all things owe their existence to the unbroken wholeness – an unending process of constant flux Bohm terms 'the holomovement'. Bohm believes, instead, that the universe is more like a total organism in which the parts only make sense in relation to the whole.

It is Bohm's emphasis on wholeness which links his conceptual framework to that of Pribram for, at a fundamental level, according to Bohm, individual consciousness has to be part of a total, universal consciousness – intelligence at its most profound level being grounded in the holomovement. Unfortunately, by using lenses and other optical equipment in scientific measurement and evaluation, we have developed a science that focuses on specific aspects of the manifested universe, rather than the greater reality of the holomovement itself.

Pribram, meanwhile, notes that in the same way that holograms are produced without lenses, it is similarly important to ask what 'reality' would look like if we did not utilise the lenses in our eyes. Lenses, he argues, produce their own sort of reality: they filter through a specific type of perception. In his essay 'The Holographic Hypothesis of Brain Function' Pribram writes:

> The importance of holonomic reality is that it constitutes what David Bohm calls an 'enfolded' or 'implicate order', which . . . is also a distributed order. Everything is enfolded into everything else and distributed all over the system. What we do with our sense organs and telescopes – lenses in general – is to explicate, to unfold that enfolded order. Our telescopes and microscopes are even called 'objectives'. That is how we explicate things: we make objects out of them with the lenses in our senses. Not only the eye, but also the skin and the ear are lens-like structures. We owe to David Bohm the conceptualisation that there is an order in the universe – the enfolded order – which is spaceless and timeless in the sense that both space and time are enfolded in it. We now find that an important aspect of brain function is also accomplished in the holonomic domain. . . .But this holonomic order is not empty; it is a boundariless plenum filling and flowing. Discovery of these characteristics of the holonomic order in physics and the brain sciences has intrigued mystics and scholars steeped in the esoteric traditions of East and West: for is not this just what they have been experiencing all along?[13]

The implications of Pribram's and Bohm's approach to the brain and consciousness are far-reaching. We begin to understand that at a core level everything in the universe is interconnected, that individual consciousness is an illusion; that the fiction we know as individual consciousness contains in essence all the potentials of universal consciousness; that the 'reality' we are so convinced of represents perhaps one small part of a much larger spectrum which we cannot adequately tune into with our existing and undoubtedly limited mental apparatus. Also, it becomes clear that reality as such is not 'fixed' as we have always assumed but is constructed by our brains so we can make sense of it.

Because the Human Potential Movement has as one of its primary tasks the unravelling of the mysteries of consciousness, Pribram's and Bohm's findings are of major importance. But at the same time the field of enquiry itself becomes much broader, encompassing not only physics and psychology but also areas traditionally associated with religion, metaphysics and mysticism. At a more general level these are also the preoccupations of the New Age.

Advocates of both the Human Potential Movement and the New Age emphasise the importance of exploring new states of being, of developing new terminologies for describing non-ordinary realms of consciousness. This journey inevitably takes us beyond fixed belief systems, beyond statements of faith, towards broader dimensions of experience. It is a quest that begins to transcend familiar frameworks of religion and which encompasses the furthest reaches of psychology – integrating the physical, mental and spiritual aspects of our being with the aim of achieving a universal, sacred gnosis. The new consciousness is very much an adventure of self-transformation which eventually takes us beyond self itself. It is a journey towards wholeness, towards totality of being.

However, the rise of the Human Potential Movement has been a steadily unfolding process which owes much to those pioneers of psychology who first began to study consciousness in the West. To relate this process we must return again to the beginning.

13

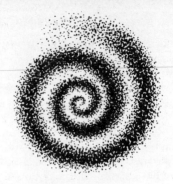

2·PIONEERS
OF HUMAN
POTENTIAL

As suggested earlier, one can argue that psychology should have been about consciousness all along. The New Age Movement, and also its more academic counterpart, the Human Potential Movement, are both preoccupied with an emphasis on consciousness rather than behaviour. Both are similarly eclectic in drawing on a range of body/mind systems for modifying or expanding consciousness, embracing as they do Eastern and Western techniques of meditation and visualisation, yoga-based breathing and bodywork methods, Zen approaches to transcending linear thinking, Taoist metaphors like *Yin* and *Yang* to express the universal flux, and so on.

At the heart of the Human Potential Movement is the recognition that consciousness – and, by extension, personal experience – has to be the starting point if we are to have any meaningful glimpses into what life is all about.

And, at a more popular level, if we regard the New Age as a blend of applied psychology coupled with a diverse assortment of metaphysical and mystical belief systems, then it is obvious that we need to consider those pioneers of modern psychology who have helped shape the current perspective.

There is no doubt that both the Human Potential Movement and the New Age alike have been strongly influenced by such thinkers as William James, Sigmund Freud, Carl Jung, Alfred Adler and Wilhelm Reich.

WILLIAM JAMES (1842–1910)

William James is not only one of the towering figures of American psychology but he also helped pioneer the study of consciousness prior to the advent of Freudian psychoanalysis and behaviourism.

James' interests were especially far-ranging. He taught anatomy, psychology and philosophy at Harvard University, explored the consequences of pragmatism as an aspect of personal belief, and was interested in a wide spectrum of unusual states – from religious and drug-induced ecstasy to psychic and spiritualist phenomena. James also summarised the aims of psychology in 1892 in terms that sound completely modern, defining it as 'the description and explanation of states of consciousness'.[1]

For William James, individual consciousness was a process of continuous thought but, unlike David Bohm and Karl Pribram he did not conceive of consciousness as a quality of the universe as a whole – for him consciousness could not be considered independently of its owner. However, he was well aware of what we now refer to as a *spectrum* of consciousness. 'Our normal waking consciousness,' he wrote, ' . . .is but one special type of consciousness whilst all about it, parted from it by the filmiest of screens, there lie potential forms of consciousness entirely different.'[2]

Elsewhere he sounds distinctly mystical in his evaluation of consciousness: ' . . .there is a continuum of cosmic conscious- ness, against which our individuality builds but accidental fences, and into which our several minds plunge as into a mother-sea or reservoir'.[3]

However, it is not only in his definitions that one finds a resonance with New Age thinking. James emphasised the importance of personal self-improvement, which is also a characteristic of the contemporary movement. James felt that any person had an innate ability to modify or adapt his or her behaviour, thereby 'evolving' to new levels of personal attainment. He also felt that a positive attitude was necessary for mental good health – a viewpoint now considered axiomatic in holistic health practices – and believed, like Sigmund Freud and Wilhelm Reich after him, that blocking emotional energy could result in illness.

Keen on a self-help orientation, William James believed that the will was essential to personal growth, describing it as 'the pivotal point from which meaningful action can occur'.[4] Will, as an expression of mental perception, enabled the human mind to 'engender truth upon reality' and thereby have a worthwhile impact upon the world at large. To this extent, then, William James felt we should all learn to develop our willpower. 'Willing orients consciousness' he wrote, 'so that a desired action can unfold of its own accord.'[5]

The emotional aspects of human consciousness, on the other hand, held a somewhat less exalted position in James' psychological schema. He felt that there should be a balance between passionately expressing one's feelings and retaining a sense of almost clinical detachment from them -- a distinction we might now correlate with right- and left-brain consciousness. James quoted Hannah Smith, who said of the emotions, 'They are not the indicators of your spiritual state but are merely the indicators of your temperament or of your present physical condition'.[6] James was well aware that emotional expressions could become excessive, or obsessive. He noted that an excess of love, for example, could manifest as possessiveness, an excess of loyalty become fanaticism, an excess of concern become sentimentality. Such apparent virtues, he believed, 'diminished' the person concerned, when expressed in an extreme form.

While on this particular point James parts company with the more hedonistic aspects of the New Age, personified for example by Bhagwan Shree Rajneesh's former ashram practices in Oregon, James nevertheless anticipates the New Age in several other ways. He distinguished three aspects of the self – the material self (physical body/home/family, and so on) from the social self (social roles and recognition) and the spiritual self (inner being) – thereby foreshadowing the much later emphasis in transpersonal psychology on spiritual factors in human wellbeing. For him the reality of one's inner self was paramount. The body, he felt, was an expressive tool of the indwelling consciousness, rather than the source of stimulation itself.[7] He also advocated what would now be called 'imaging' or 'creative visualisation' in the New Age – the technique of holding images in one's mind in order to train and develop the will.

So, in several ways, we can consider William James an important forerunner of the New Age movement. While many psychologists since his time have been essentially reductionist in their orientation, seeking to reduce the subtleties of perception and brain functioning to basic biological activity, James was aware that consciousness itself poses a mystery, that there could well be much broader domains of causality than those normally accessed by the human organism in the everyday world:

> The whole drift of my education goes to persuade me that the world of our present consciousness is only one of many worlds of consciousness that exist, and that those other worlds must contain experiences which have a meaning for our life also; and that although in the main their experiences and those of this world keep discrete, yet the two become continuous at certain points and higher energies filter in.[8]

SIGMUND FREUD (1856–1939)

These days it has become fashionable to denigrate Sigmund Freud, to summarily dismiss him as being obsessed with explaining the very complex and multi-faceted aspects of personality primarily in terms of sexuality. While there is some truth in this assessment – Freud always stuck to his original position that sexuality in its various aspects is the central problem underlying psychological adjustment – his contribution to modern thought is much greater than this.

It is easy to forget that Freud was the first person in Western psychology to emphasise the importance of the unconscious mind, to systematise the study of dreams, and to distinguish certain elementary instincts. And while Freudian psychotherapy often seems heavily laden with analytical concepts it is also important to remember that Freud did not simply dwell on repressed sexuality and other aspects of neurosis for their own sake. In Freud's view, the essential task of the therapist, in aiding the process of personal growth, was to help the patient recover and reintegrate material from the unconscious mind, in short, to help that person's life to be more balanced and satisfying. The final intent of Freud's psychology, then, has always been positive and integrative and, to this extent, optimistic. Ilham Dilman, a noted interpreter of Freud, has also confirmed this position. In Freudian terms, he writes, coming to self-knowledge, or discovering who one *is*, is to become what one was not before. 'It is not only the shedding of screens, but also the integration of what is old, and the assimilation of what is new.'[9]

Like William James, Freud also believed that the starting point in psychology was consciousness, although the conscious itself was only a small part of the mind. Freud was especially interested in the less familiar areas of the mind, which he termed the 'pre-conscious' – representing areas like immediate memories, readily accessible to consciousness – and the 'unconscious', that vast pool of non-conscious material including instincts and repressed memories.

17

Early on, Freud considered erotic and physically gratifying sexual instincts and aggressive, destructive instincts to be the two main impulses of human life. He later changed his emphasis, contrasting life-supporting and life-denying instincts as unresolved polarities in human nature. He conceived of a conscious *ego* welling up from a formless, unorganised *id* representing a kind of 'reservoir of energy for the whole personality'.[10] The life-instinct, or *libido*, he tended to equate with sexual energy: a support for the ego in its quest to pursue pleasure and self-preservation. Freud also formulated his idea of the *super-ego* as a censor to the ego, inhibiting unwelcome thoughts and providing a sense of morality or conscience. In this sense the super-ego was a restrictive overseer of voluntary actions.

According to Freud, however, the unconscious contents of the mind only remained unconscious at the expense of a considerable amount of libidinal energy. He also believed that the dramatic release of pent-up energies invariably provided a sense of 'explosive satisfaction'.[11] In making this observation, Freud influenced both Wilhelm Reich and, in turn, many forms of contemporary New Age bodywork which tend to regard the body's musculature as a repository of stored tension and sexual repression. Freud's insight also underlies the development of modern cathartic approaches to mind and body like Bioenergetics, which help to move subjects past barriers of blocked emotion and provide a supportive setting for releasing these energies in a dramatic outpouring. We will encounter these therapies again, and discuss them in more detail, later in this book.

Freud emphasised that energy could be rechannelled from essentially sexual or aggressive goals towards artistic, intellectual or cultural pursuits, but he believed that, in essence, human beings are not the rational animals they think they are. Instead, he regarded them as creatures driven by powerful emotional forces which were unconscious in origin – the restriction of these forces invariably leading to neurosis, suffering and pain.

Freud liked to believe in a world where, ideally, the rational ego could rise up and overcome the irrational id – he once declared, 'Where id is, there let ego be'[12] – but he also felt that there were no psychological accidents in human behaviour. Our choice of friends, locations, favourite foods, recreational pastimes – all of these were linked to unconscious memories, and in turn provided clues towards a rationale of our conscious lives. The essential task, then, was to further self-knowledge by probing as far as possible into the contents of the unconscious mind.

Freud developed psychoanalysis specifically with this purpose in mind. It was intended 'to liberate previously inaccessible unconscious materials so that they may be dealt with consciously',[13] thereby enabling people to be freed from the suffering they in some way perpetually bring upon themselves.

The idea that we cause our own suffering, and, by extension, that we are to blame for the diseases we inflict upon ourselves, is also very much a New Age belief. In a manner which blends Freud and the Hindu concept of karma, it is now fashionable to emphasise that we each 'create our own reality' and should in turn 'take the responsibility' to liberate ourselves from the shortcomings we have unconsciously 'chosen'. This is Freud simplified to the point of a cliché, but nevertheless expressed in a manner which is easy to understand. It also aligns with Freud's notion that the practical goal of psychoanalysis is to strengthen the ego, to eliminate the unconscious blocks which cause self-destructive behaviour. The Freudian idea of personal growth is therefore to reclaim one's life-energy from the grips of the unconscious. As Dilman puts it, 'A neurotic who has been cured has really become a different person, although at bottom of course he remains the same – that is, he has become his best self, what he would have been under the most favourable conditions.' The analyst aims to bring about the change by 'making conscious the unconscious, removing repressions (and) filling in the gaps in memory'.[14]

According to Freud, one of the most important pathways to one's unconscious energies was through analysing the contents of dreams. Dreams, said Freud, provided 'the royal road to a knowledge of the unconscious'. Freud's first major publication was a work still regarded by many as his most enduring, *The Interpretation of Dreams* (1900). It was this book which first drew Jung into Freud's circle and which also made a strong impression on Alfred Adler, Otto Rank and Ernest Jones, all early members of Freud's psychoanalytic movement.

Freud had originally believed that dreams were a garbled expression of mental events but after formulating the concept of the id in 1897 Freud subsequently maintained that we all dream because the id yearns for self-expression. Sleep relaxes the ego's censoring control of the unconscious, allowing all manner of fantasies and wish-fulfilments to rise up. For Freud, every dream, even a nightmare or anxiety dream, was an attempt to fulfil a wish, and these wish-fulfilments could stem as much from early childhood as current daily events. Freud also noted that in neurotic behaviour – and who wasn't neurotic in late nineteenth century Vienna? – sexuality was invariably associated with repressed or suppressed wishes. All of these patterns one could uncover through dream analysis, or, as Freud termed it, 'dream-work'.

During sleep the dreamer's mind would find expression in dreams. Freud therefore developed the technique of afterwards talking his patients through their dreams, heeding their own 'free association' of ideas and memories, and then scrutinising the dream reports in detail. Basically, Freud believed that dreams help the psyche to protect and satisfy itself, channelling previously unfulfilled desires through to awareness without arousing the resting physical body. Dreams could therefore be seen as a way of playing out fantasies which could not be fulfilled during the day. It was intriguing how often dreams allowed a person to overstep boundaries of conventional morality, but this in turn was a key to understanding their role: dreams were able to help release tension because the id made no distinction between the resolution of needs in the physical, sensory world or the dream-world.

Although dreams often appeared jumbled and distorted, Freud showed that they could be unravelled and decoded. However, he was somewhat inclined to look for recurring motifs in dreams, with specific connotations. Symbols usually represented the human body in some way – long stiff objects equating with the penis, hair-cutting with castration, boxes and chests with the womb, walking up and down steps with coitus, and so on – and the dreams were symbolic expressions of sex-wishes.[15] It was here, in particular, that he would later part company with Carl Jung, whose analysis of dreams, as we shall see shortly, had quite a different emphasis.

Nevertheless, Freud was the first person to undertake the enormous task of unravelling the contents of the unconscious mind and it is this, more than anything, which aligns him in spirit with the intent of the New Age. Even if some of his conclusions were overstated and his themes of sexuality perhaps over-emphasised, Freud towers over the landscape as a pioneer of consciousness exploration. And without doubt, his contribution to our understanding of the inner world of the psyche owes much to his evaluation of dreams. As Freud wrote in 1900:

> Dreams are not to be likened to the unregulated sounds that rise from a musical instrument struck by the blow of some external force instead of a player's hand; they are not meaningless; they are not absurd; they do not imply that one portion of our store of ideas is asleep

while another portion is beginning to wake. On the contrary, they are psychical phenomena of complete validity – fulfilment of wishes; they can be inserted into the chain of intelligible waking mental acts; they are constructed by a highly complicated activity of the mind.[16]

CARL JUNG (1875–1961)

Sigmund Freud had a substantial influence on Jung, and *The Interpretation of Dreams* stimulated Jung's own forays into dream analysis. As Jung was moved to say of Freud: 'By evaluating dreams as the most important source of information concerning the unconscious processes, he gave back to mankind a tool that had seemed irretrievably lost.'[17] Nevertheless, while Jung accepted the Freudian concept of a personal unconscious he soon began to conceive of a broader-based 'collective' unconscious which transcended the individual psyche. He also found himself increasingly dissatisfied with Freud's model of sexual repression and made the final split with him in 1912, following the publication of *Symbols of Transformation*, which rejected the sexual libido.

For Jung the unconscious seemed to contain a vast storehouse of imagery which was much greater than the repressions of the individual. It also seemed to him that to a certain extent the unconscious appeared to act independently of the conscious mind. In addition, Jung began to move away from Freud's original approach to dream analysis, relying less and less on the 'free association' technique. Gradually he came to the view that to allow the patient to discuss dreams at random would entail moving away from the dream itself. For him each dream was complete within itself and 'expressed something specific that the unconscious was trying to say'. Whereas Freud invariably tended to uncover sexual motifs in dreams, Jung regarded the individual situation as foremost in solving the language of the dream, rather than attempting to identify fixed motifs like the penis or breast. Jung emphasised this point when he wrote:

A man may dream of inserting a key in a lock, of wielding a heavy stick, or of breaking down a door with a battering ram. Each of these can be regarded as a sexual allegory. But the fact that his unconscious, for its own purposes, has chosen one of these specific images – it may be the key, the stick or the battering ram – is also of major significance. The real task is to understand why the key has been preferred to the stick or the stick to the ram. And sometimes this might even lead one to

21

Carl Jung – dreams expressed something specific that the unconscious was
trying to say (Credit: *The Australian*)

discover that it is not the sexual act at all that is represented but some
quite different psychological point.[18]

Jung concluded that the dream had 'its own limitation' and could
not be manipulated so that a symbol meant the same thing in every
dream. Nevertheless the dream was not a random occurrence but
intrinsically made sense, if only its meaning could be discovered.
The dream was 'a specific expression of the unconscious',[19] and
the reason why it was expressed at all, said Jung, was that it was
compensating for aspects of the personality which were unbalanced.

22

An over-egotistical person would frequently have dreams about symbolically 'coming down to earth', for example.

But there were also certain motifs within dreams which did not seem to Jung to be a part of the individual psyche. It was the study of these symbols which led him to formulate the concept of the 'collective unconscious'. He wrote:

> There are many symbols that are not individual but collective in their nature and origin. These are chiefly religious images; their origin is so far buried in the mystery of the past that they seem to have no human source. But they are, in fact, 'collective representations' emanating from primeval dreams and creative fantasies. As such, these images are involuntary spontaneous manifestations and by no means intentional inventions.[20]

What Jung was saying, in effect, was that at a certain psychic level, motifs common to the whole of mankind were capable of manifesting in dreams. These motifs were a symbolic expression of 'the constantly repeated experiences of humanity'. That is to say, they were derived from observations about nature (the sky, changes of the seasons, and so on) which had become embedded in the psychic patterns of the whole human species.

Jung called these primordial images 'archetypes' and gives the following example of how an archetype is formed:

> One of the commonest and at the same time most impressive experiences is the apparent movement of the sun every day. We certainly cannot discover anything of the kind in the unconscious, so far as the known physical process is concerned. What we do find, on the other hand, is the myth of the sun hero in all its countless modifications. It is this *myth* and *not the physical process* that forms the sun archetype.[21]

Thus the archetype may take the form of an anthropomorphic rendition of a force in nature. Its potency derives from the fact that the observation of the sun's movement constitutes one of the universal, fundamental experiences of existence, and is something which man cannot change, a power beyond man's manipulation. The sun becomes an object of veneration, and mystically one of a number of archetypes with which to identify in religious or ritual acts of transcendence. Naturally, different cultures would conceive

23

of the sun-hero in a different form (for example, Apollo-Helios in Greece and Rome, Ohrmazd in ancient Persia) because traditions and styles colour our various conceptions, but Jung regarded all of these as patterns on a theme – the core common to all of these representations being, in this instance, the archetypal sun-god himself. But apart from its universality there was another side to the archetype, its awe-inspiring vibrancy and its apparent autonomy, or ability to appear separate. As Jung notes:

> The 'primordial images', or archetypes, lead their own independent life. . . as can easily be seen in those philosophical or gnostic systems which rely on awareness of the unconscious as the source of knowledge. The idea of angels, archangels, 'principalities and powers' in St Paul, the archons of the Gnostics, the heavenly hierarchy of Dionysius the Areopagite, all come from the perception of the relative *autonomy* of the archetypes.[22]

Furthermore, said Jung, an archetype contains within it a certain type of power or influence: 'It seizes hold of the psyche with a kind of primeval force.'[23]

Over the years, and especially with the development of the idea of archetypes, a clear tendency began to emerge in Jung's thinking which differentiated him markedly from Freud. Jung considered the deepest regions of the psyche to be profoundly spiritual, whereas Freud's concept of the id suggested formlessness or chaos. Increasingly, Jung came to the view that the essential aim of personal growth was to move towards a state of wholeness by integrating the conflicting contents and archetypal processes of the unconscious: he called this process *individuation*.

Jung distinguished different aspects of the personality. These included the *persona*, the face we use to present ourselves to the world, and the *ego*, which included all the conscious contents of personal experience. However Jung also believed that men and women should accommodate opposite gender polarities within their consciousness – he termed these the *anima* for men and the *animus* for women – and he talked of the *shadow*, an embodiment of memories and experiences repressed from consciousness altogether. The shadow would often appear in dreams and nightmares as a dark, repellent figure. Jung argued, however, that if material from the shadow was acknowledged and allowed back into consciousness, that much of its dark, frightening nature would disappear. Dealing with the dark side of the psyche remains an important aspect of all Jungian forms of psychotherapy.

Jung regarded the *self* as the totality of the personality, including all the aspects of the psyche mentioned above. He also considered the self to be a central archetype, personified symbolically by a circle or mandala, representations of wholeness. The thrust of all individual self-development was therefore towards wholeness of being. Self-realisation, or individuation, simply meant 'becoming oneself' in a true and total sense.

Jung described the process of personal growth in his essay 'The Relations Between the Ego and the Unconscious' (1928):

> The more we become conscious of ourselves through self-knowledge, and act accordingly, the more the layer of the personal unconscious that is superimposed on the collective unconscious will be diminished. In this way there arises a consciousness which is no longer imprisoned in the petty, oversensitive, personal world of objective interests. This widened consciousness is no longer that touchy, egotistical bundle of personal wishes, fears, hopes and ambitions which always has to be compensated or corrected by unconscious countertendencies; instead, it is a function of relationship to the world of objects, bringing the individual into absolute, binding and indissoluble communion with the world at large.[24]

Jung's impact on New Age thinking has been enormous, greater, perhaps, than many people realise. Jung emphasised dreams as living realities – direct communications from the psyche – and we find the idea of heeding the inner voice not only in New Age dream workshops, but as a broad-based principle underlying the widespread resurgence of inner-directed growth and visualisation techniques in general. Jung also believed that *spontaneous* manifestations of the psyche were most important, and this is reflected in the free-form sketch-drawings of psychic and spiritual states which feature so prominently in many New Age workshops.

Meanwhile, Jung's idea of a collective unconscious has also encouraged many to look at myths, fables and legends for insights into the human condition, and also to relate the cycles of symbolic rebirth, found in many of the world's major religions, to the process of personal individuation.

Jung's focus is undoubtedly on *individual* transformation, although obviously the individuation process broadens through relationships with other people. Nevertheless, Jung's orientation reinforces a commonly held New Age perception that one must work on oneself first, before expanding the process of self-development to include others – otherwise it is simply a matter of the blind leading the blind.

In the final analysis Jung is saying that we hold our spiritual destinies in our own hands. The archetypes of the collective unconscious provide spiritual milestones along the profound and awe-inspiring pathway which leads to the reintegration of the psyche. Where this journey takes us is really up to us.

ALFRED ADLER (1870–1937)

Alder's formulation of Individual Psychology, like Jung's concept of individuation, has similarly had a major impact on humanistic psychology, and this impact in turn has flowed on to the Human Potential and New Age Movements.

Adler's thinking, reinforced by various childhood tragedies and struggles in his own life, focuses heavily on the notion of self-improvement. For Adler, the task of all healthy, motivated individuals was to develop their own capacities and potential. As Adler himself wrote, 'The striving for perfection is innate, in the sense that it is part of life. . .'[25]

Adler accepted Darwin's idea of living forms adapting to the environment and he conceived of what he termed 'life-goals' as a focus for individual achievement in their efforts to overcome life's obstacles. Life goals, he believed, generally served as a defence against feelings of impotence, as a bridge from the unsatisfying present to a bright, powerful and fulfilling future.[26]

Adler emphasised individualism even more than Jung, ascribing to individual human beings such qualities as uniqueness, genuine awareness and the ability to take control of their own lives – aspects he felt Freud had down-played. Adler was convinced, in fact, that we can mould our own personalities and to this extent he championed a belief which has continued, in force, in the New Age.

'Every individual', said Adler, 'represents both a unity of personality and the individual fashioning of that unity. The individual is thus both the picture and the artist. He is the artist of his own personality.'[27]

Nevertheless, while one can find considerable support in his writings for the idea of developing human potential, Adler was more inclined than Jung to express this endeavour in a social context. For Adler, all human behaviour was ultimately *social* – one had to develop a sense of fellowship within the community, a feeling of kinship which ultimately would embrace all humanity. Adler thus moved the emphasis from individual self-growth towards contributing to the community at a large:

> Psychological growth is primarily a matter of moving from a self-centred attitude and the goal of personal superiority to an attitude of constructive mastery of the environment and socially useful development. Constructive striving for superiority plus strong social interest and co-operation are the basic traits of the healthy individual.[28]

It is worth noting that Adler was also influenced by two other philosophers who in turn held views compatible with New Age thought. The first of these was Hans Vaihinger, the other Jan Smuts. Vaihinger subscribed to the interesting view that people are more affected by their future expectations in life than they are by past experiences – a completely different emphasis from Freud's. According to Vaihinger, human behaviour is thus a type of fiction based on personal conceptualisations of the world. Vaihinger's idea influenced Adler's concept of life-goals and is also reflected in the New Age dictum that the way we see ourselves is what we become: that ultimately our thoughts create our reality.

The other influence on Adler was Jan Smuts, the distinguished statesman and field-marshal who became Premier of the Union of South Africa for two periods, between 1919 and 1948. Aside from his military and political career, Smuts was deeply interested in science and philosophy and he produced a book titled *Holism and Evolution*. Here he took the unorthodox scientific view that there is a tendency in nature to produce wholes which are not explicable in terms of the sum of their parts. According to Smuts there was an impulse always towards greater organisation in nature and in all individuals an innate movement towards wholeness.

Adler and Smuts corresponded with each other and Adler made holism an integral part of his Individual Psychology, defining the self as the personality viewed as an integrated whole. Adler believed that we should regard each individual as a unified being. He wrote: 'The foremost task of Individual Psychology is to prove this unity in each individual – in his thinking, feeling, acting; in his so-called conscious and unconscious – in every expression of his personality.'[29]

27

WILHELM REICH (1897–1957)

Of the early pioneers of the Human Potential Movement acknowledgement, too, must be made to Wilhelm Reich. Reich's concepts of sexual energy and body armouring continue to have a major impact on contemporary holistic bodywork practices and Reich himself represents a tangible link between the early days of Freudian psychoanalysis and body/mind frameworks adopted by the New Age.

Reich studied at the University of Vienna, qualifying as an MD in 1922. Reich then went to work with Sigmund Freud in his psychoanalysis clinic. However, as with Jung and Adler before him, Reich soon began to differ from Freud and a rift developed between them. Freud refused to give Reich personal analysis and did not share the latter's strong Marxist leanings. Nevertheless, a strongly Freudian flavour characterises much of Reich's thinking on sexual energy, although Reich developed his theories especially in relation to the body, rather than to the mind.

Reich believed in the concept of 'bioenergy flow' through the body and considered that repression of the emotions and sexual instincts could lead to 'blockages' resulting in rigid patterns of behaviour (character armour) and the tightening of specific muscle groups (body armour). As such blockages increased, the energy flow in the organism was impeded and in chronic instances would lead to a marked deterioration of health.

For Reich, as for Freud, sexual energy was the essence of human existence. The climax of orgasm was a completely satisfying release from tension that allowed sexual energy to be discharged in an act of physical embrace and love. Reich later postulated his formula of 'biological tension and charge' which involved four stages: mechanical tension, bioenergetic charge, bioenergetic discharge and relaxation. He noted, too, that the full orgasm had an almost transcendent quality, involving loss of ego and a profound sense of peace. By contrast, people who felt guilty in sexual expression worked against the current of bioenergy or 'orgone energy' as he called it, and produced frustrations and emotions that were subsequently repressed. This brought with it the neurotic, negative behaviour that Reich termed 'character armouring'. Sexual energy produced an effect on the autonomic nervous system which, in turn via sympathetic and parasympathetic actions, caused a tangible influence on specific organs in the body. While a healthy organism would normally exhibit patterns of contraction and expansion – a type of rhythm of life – in the case of an 'armoured' organism there was a permanent state of contraction. Reich was appalled by the fact that mass neurosis appeared to be the norm in Western society and believed that such character patterns derived primarily from defences against the free flow of sexual energy.

In essence Reich's therapy is a dismantling of layers of pent up emotion. Reich divided the body into seven zones at right angles to the spine and centred in the eyes, mouth, neck, chest, diaphragm, abdomen and pelvis (including the legs). He believed that orgone energy was bound up in chronic muscular spasms and that it was necessary to free this energy progressively. Reichian 'bodywork' therapy entails dissolving the armour, beginning with the eyes and working down the body. Several approaches are used:

Deep breathing   Breathing conforms to patterns proposed by the therapist. The patient may feel the stream of bioenergy in the form of prickling or tingling sensations.

Deep massage   Pressure is applied to muscle spasms. Sometimes such areas of tension are pinched to loosen them up.

Facial expressions   The patient 'makes faces' expressing certain emotions while keeping eye contact with the therapist and maintaining certain patterns of breathing.

Chest-work   The therapist pushes down on the chest while the patient exhales or screams. Such bodywork is designed to remove blockages to breathing.

Convulsive reflex-work   Convulsions break down armouring. The therapist may work with the disruptive effects of coughing, yawning, and so on.

Stress positions   Stress positions may be maintained to produce an effect of bodily irritation. This may lead in turn to tremors or 'clonisms' which similarly break down the body armour.

29

Active movements   The therapist may encourage the patient to kick and stamp and move parts of the body vigorously, as a 'loosening up' exercise.

In general, Reichian therapy penetrates from outer, accessible layers of armouring to deeper and deeper levels. It is important that such probing occur at a pace that the patient can handle. Different effects are noted in each of the body segments:

The eyes   The eyes may appear dull and lifeless. The patient is encouraged to roll them from side to side and perhaps open them wide, as if in a state of sudden amazement.

The mouth   This area includes the muscles of the chin, throat and back of the head. The patient may be asked to cry, shout or suck, or move the lips in various ways, in order to loosen up the muscles concerned.

The neck   Screaming and yelling may be used to free up tensions here also.

The chest   Any armouring here will show up when the patient breathes or laughs. Inhibition of breathing is a means of suppressing the emotions and may require the use of special gestures involving the arms and hands.

The diaphragm   Armouring tends to reveal itself via body posture in this segment. The spine may curve forward, constricting outward breath. Such armouring is loosened with breathing exercises and the so-called 'gag reflex'.

The abdomen   This segment includes the back and abdominal muscles which are often tense if a person is defensive. Armouring is loosened up in these muscle regions.

The pelvis and lower limbs   With strong armouring the pelvis is pulled back and may stick out, revealing signs of deep-seated repressed anxiety. There is also a tightening of the pelvis, inhibiting sexual expression and pleasure. The patient may be asked to strike the couch with the pelvis region or kick the feet until a sense of freedom in this region develops.

Reichian therapy thus provides a systematic loosening of body tensions aimed at releasing the natural flow of energy through the body, and in this way does for the body what Freudian psychoanalysis intends to do for the mind. Indeed, Reich's approach has been a major influence on bodywork therapies like Bioenergetics, Rolfing and the Feldenkrais method of body awareness and movement, all modalities which have played a distinctive role in the Human Potential Movement and in holistic health in general.

Reichian therapy provides a classic example of the fact that the work first undertaken by Freud and the other early twentieth century pioneers of psychology continues to flow through to the New Consciousness today.

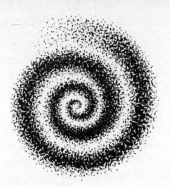

3·TOWARDS THE TRANSPERSONAL

While Wilhelm Reich's contribution to bodywork provides a specific link between the early schools of psychology and the rise of New Age consciousness, another development in psychology also had a major role to play. This was the emergence of the 'Humanistic' school and its possibly even more important offshoot, the Transpersonal perspective.

It is popular these days to talk of Transpersonal psychology as the 'Fourth Force' following Freudian psychoanalysis, Behaviourism and Humanistic psychology. As its name suggests, Transpersonal psychology refers to states of being beyond the ego. The Transpersonal perspective seeks to broaden the traditional scope of psychological enquiry, taking in such studies as the nature of holistic wellbeing, peak religious and mystical experiences, the experiential psychotherapies and the wisdom traditions of East and West.

Humanistic and Transpersonal psychology both owe their development to two key figures: Abraham Maslow (1908–70) and Anthony J. Sutich (1907–76). Their personal interest in spiritual values as part of the ultimate definition of a human being led historically to a perspective which is now blossoming on a more popular level in the New Age.

Abraham Maslow was appointed to the Chair of Psychology at Brandeis University in 1952 and was strongly opposed to the

Behaviouristic frameworks which dominated in most American psychology departments at that time. It is interesting to note that in 1954 he began to develop a mailing list of other psychologists around the country who shared his interests – these were people concerned with such issues as creativity, love, self-actualisation and personal growth in human beings. Three years later the list still comprised fewer than 125 people!

Maslow's personal orientation drew on cultural anthropology and neuropsychiatry, but he was also influenced by Gestalt psychology and was strongly holistic in his approach. Like Jung and Adler before him, he emphasised that the human organism should be viewed in terms of its total potential.

As a result, Maslow developed his well-known 'hierarchy of needs', which included physiological considerations like hunger and sleep; safety (stability and order); belonging and love (family and friendship) and esteem (self-respect and recognition). Maslow's hierarchy culminated in the need for self-actualisation, or, as he defined it, 'the full use and exploitation of talents, capacities [and] potentialities'.[1] He was also very interested in the sorts of people capable of self-actualisation. Maslow found that such people tended to be spontaneous and independent in their natures, given to deep interpersonal relations, democratic in their character, creative in their approach to life, and able to rise above cultural limitations. He also found that self-actualisers often had the ability to have mystical or peak experiences.

Maslow's particular research focus was to evaluate people who seemed healthy and creative, rather than those who were unhealthy or neurotic. Maslow felt that unhealthy, psychologically unbalanced or maladjusted people did not provide adequate research data relating to the true nature of human potential in terms of personal growth. On the other hand, self-actualisation had everything to do with personal growth. According to Maslow it was vital that we transcend the distorting images we have of ourselves and overcome the defence mechanisms we develop which hide the *real* person inside. As Maslow noted: 'One cannot choose wisely for a life unless he dares to listen to himself, *his own self*, at each moment in life. . .'[2]

The other key figure in the emergence of Humanistic and Transpersonal psychology, as mentioned earlier, was Anthony Sutich. Sutich was not an academic in the strict sense of the word – he would come to think of himself in due course as a 'maverick psychotherapist' – but he brought to the new orientation a profound interest in spiritual and mystical concerns.

Sutich had developed progressive rheumatoid arthritis following an accident in a baseball game when he was 12 years old. By the time he was 18, he was totally physically disabled and his formal education had to finish in grade nine. The remainder of his life would be spent for the most part on a gurney – a four-wheeled stretcher fitted with a telephone, reading stand and other devices.

Nevertheless, despite his physical disability, Sutich continued to function very effectively. He would often talk with nursing staff about their personal problems and soon acquired a reputation as a trusted friend and counsellor. For many years people would come to him in hospital seeking advice, and in 1938 he was asked to become a group counsellor for the Pala Alto Society for the Blind. In 1941 he began a full-time private practice in both individual and group counselling.

In due course Sutich became involved in political and social issues related to the labour movement and also worked as a Serbo-Croatian translator for the State Department during World War II. However he also had a long-standing interest in both Western and Eastern religion – especially the latter. He read widely in the fields of Yoga, Vedanta, Theosophy and Christian Science. He had a personal interest, too, in psychedelic and mystical states of consciousness, and, as he wrote in a dissertation presented shortly before his death, 'I myself had had a mystical experience, or something like one, several times, with and without psychedelic substances, as early as 1935'.[3]

Sutich was especially impressed by Swami Ashokananda of the San Francisco Vedanta Society, who emphasised in his lectures 'the strong case for the value and validity of scientific investigation directed toward the inner realm of human potentialities, especially the spiritual potential'.[4]

Sutich was already familiar with the works of Swami Ramakrishna and Swami Vivekananda, and after having adjustments made to his car to accommodate his physical disability was able to travel to psychology and mysticism seminars in person. In the summer of 1948 he attended a series of lectures by Krishnamurti at Ojai, California. However he found Krishnamurti's 'vague generalities about "Reality"' disappointing. 'He struck me as a cold, detached, rather negative person', wrote Sutich later. 'It was his lack of warmth and humourless manner that made me feel that something was lacking in Eastern mysticism.'[5]

Sutich's interest in mysticism was rekindled, however, by reading Swami Akhilananda's *Hindu Psychology*, while at the same time he began to feel increasingly alienated by the rising wave of Behavioural psychology at nearby Stanford University. Sutich would often test the attitudes and expressions of his clients and he began to think very much in terms of their 'psychological growth'. However, few of his colleagues used terms like this in their practices. Sutich was particularly keen on group therapy which emphasised spiritual as well as emotional development.

Not surprisingly, Sutich was delighted when he heard about Maslow's work, and decided to write to him in November 1948 in an effort to make contact:

> I understand that you have recently been working on something that has been vaguely described to me as the 'extremely well-adjusted personal-ity'; alternatively, the 'super-normal personality'. The reference to your work came up as a result of my exploratory and experimen-tal counselling work on what I call the 'growth-centred attitude' ('growth-conscious' or 'growth-minded') as the 'core' of a 'full-valued personality'[6]

Maslow did not reply directly but in March 1949 Maslow was visiting Berkeley and one of Sutich's clients arranged for the two to meet. It was a friendly meeting and on Maslow's recommendation Sutich submitted an article to the *Journal of Psychology* titled 'The growth-experience and growth-centred attitude', which was accepted for publication.

Between 1949 and 1957 Sutich had little contact with Maslow but he did attend a lecture at Stanford University where he noted that there was strong opposition from Ernest Hilgard's Behaviourist Department of Psychology to Maslow's concept of self-actualisation. However, in 1952 Sutich met the expatriate British author Alan Watts and this lifted his spirits somewhat, once again renewing his interest in mysticism and psychotherapy. Sutich notes:

> The more I talked with him, the more I read about mysticism. In addi-tion to Watts' books I read everything in mysticism I could get hold of. This carried me into the works of Sri Aurobindo (1948), Besant (1897), Blavatsky (1927), the Bhagavad Gita (Isherwood, 1947), Muller (1899), the Upanishads (Radhakrishnan, 1953) and a variety of books dealing with yoga.[7]

Sutich subsequently began to help Watts with various counselling techniques and was intrigued when Watts said that he intended combining these methods with Zen Buddhism. Watts felt he could apply 'non-directive counselling', the main idea being 'to help those who run into certain kinds of paradoxes or contradictions'. Sutich also discussed the idea of *Satori* – the Zen concept of sudden enlightenment – with Watts in some detail.

We mentioned earlier Abraham Maslow's mailing list of like-minded psychologists. Sutich took a personal interest in this list and would later reflect upon it as the very basis of the new Humanistic psychology. 'The mailing list' he commented, 'was like the Committee on Correspondence that played such an important part in the history of the American Revolution.'[8]

However Sutich noticed that even though the mailing list was growing there were no substantial inroads against the Behaviourists, who still dominated the academic journals with their publications. Maslow, who had recently had an article on peak experiences turned down by the *Psychology Review*, urged Sutich to start a new journal. It could focus on all the aspects of human potential which were being ignored by mainstream psychology. It was proposed that the new publication be called *The Journal of Ortho-Psychology* (from the Greek *ortho*, 'to grow straight') and Maslow proposed the following statement of purpose:

> *The Journal of Ortho-Psychology* is being founded by a group of psychologists who are interested in those human capacities and poten-tialities that have no systematic place either in positivistic or behav-iouristic theory or in classical psychoanalytic theory, e.g. creativeness, love, self-actualisation, 'higher' values, ego-transcendence, objectivity, autonomy, responsibility, psychological health etc. This approach to psychology can also be characterised by the writings of Goldstein, Fromm, Horney, Rogers, Maslow, Allport, Angyal, Buhler, Moustakas etc. As well as by certain aspects of the writings of Jung, Adler and the psychoanalytic ego-psychologists.
>
> While the point of view of this 'Third Force' in psychology has not yet been synthesised, unified or systematised, nor is it yet as comprehen-sive as the Freudian or Behaviouristic systems, it is our feeling that this can come to pass, and probably soon will. . .[9]

At this time Maslow numbered among his sympathisers not only those mentioned above but also Rollo May and Gardner Murphy, both distinguished psychologists. Articles for the new journal be-gan to arrive from March 1958 onwards, and then Lewis Mumford, David Reismann and Erich Fromm joined the Board of Editors. There were difficulties with the title, however, because it clashed with *The American Journal of Orthopsychiatry*. In December 1959 Sutich received a letter from Maslow's son-in-law, Stephen Cohen, proposing that the journal be renamed *The Journal of Humanistic*

Psychology, and he was pleased with this new name. Soon after-wards, the American Association of Humanistic Psychology and the journal were established under the auspices of Brandeis University.

Around a year later, in 1962, Maslow wrote to Sutich about an excit-ing new contact he had made. Michael Murphy and his friend Richard Price had established a centre called the Esalen Institute in Big Sur, California, south of Monterey. 'They are planning a conference centre there devoted, among other topics, to just the things you are interested in' wrote Maslow. He added: 'By the way, I suggested you as a teacher to them. . .'[10]

Murphy later contacted Sutich, inviting him down as a guest once things were established. 'We are planning seminars and conferences for next fall and beyond and so are gathering ideas' wrote Murphy. 'I have written to several people already, asking them to suggest ideas and people who would be good leaders. One interest we hope to develop is the inter-disciplinary approach to human nature – getting people together who usually don't get together. . .'[11]

BEGINNINGS OF THE TRANSPERSONAL MOVEMENT

In one of his information newsletters circulated at Esalen Institute in May 1965 Michael Murphy posed a question which would become central to the Transpersonal perspective as a whole: 'What is the fundamental growth process,' he asked, 'which takes the human organism beyond its present situation into the yet unrealised poten-tial of its particular future?'[12]

Ensuing programmes at Esalen would hope to tackle this important question. In January 1966 a Humanistic Theology seminar was held at Esalen and attended by a number of Jesuit theologians as well as lead-ing humanists like James Fadiman, Willis Harman, Miles Vich and, of course, Anthony Sutich. One of the lecturers at the seminar asked the Jesuits present whether they had ever had a mystical experience and whether it was Church policy to encourage attainment of that experience. To both questions they replied 'No', and Sutich recalled that he was very surprised by these answers.[13]

Shortly after this seminar, Sutich attended two further meetings at Big Sur which highlighted the limitations of Humanistic psychology. He began to feel that the original idea of self-actualisation was no longer comprehensive enough and he expressed these views in a letter to Maslow in August 1966, noting that a humanistic therapist could hardly avoid the issue of 'ultimate goals' and mystical experi-ences. Accordingly, the therapist should also be able to assist his client in developing skills and pertinent techniques for awakening these faculties. 'Esalen and other places and processes', he added hopefully, 'may become at least the American equivalent of Zen monasteries. The Residential program that has just begun at Esalen may be a more concrete example of what may develop eventually throughout the country.'[14]

Increasingly, Sutich felt inclined to blend mysticism and Humanistic psychology. He even proposed a new term, 'Humanisticism', but Maslow pointed out that the noted British biologist Julian Huxley was already using a comparable expression, 'Trans-humanistic', with the same idea in mind. Ever keen on new publications, Sutich suggested to Maslow in February 1967 that a new journal be founded: a *Journal of Transhumanism* or *Transhumanistic Psychology*. Sutich also wrote to Huxley requesting a detailed definition of the new term.

Meanwhile on 14 September 1967, in an address to the San Francisco Unitarian Church titled 'The Farther Reaches of Human Nature', Maslow made the first reference to what he called the new 'Fourth Force', a school of psychology dedicated to the transformation of human life. Fond of delineating specific objectives Sutich proposed to Maslow a more complete definition of the new school:

> Transhumanistic (or Fourth Force) Psychology is the title given to an emerging force in the psychology field by a group of psychologists and professional men and women from other fields who are interested in those ultimate human capacities and potentialities and their actualisation that have no systematic place in either the First Force (classical psychoanalytical theory), Second Force (positivistic or behaviouristic theory), or Third Force (humanistic psychology which deals with such concepts as creativity, love, growth, basic need-gratification, psychological health, self-actualisation etc.). The emerging 'Fourth Force' is specifically concerned with the study, understanding, and responsible implementation of such states as being, becoming, self-actualisation, expression and actualisation of meta-needs (individual and 'species-wide'), ultimate values, self-transcendence, unitive consciousness, peak experiences, ecstasy, mystical experience, awe, wonder, ultimate meaning, transformation of the self, spirit, species-wide transformation, oneness, cosmic awareness, maximal sensory responsiveness, cosmic play, individual and species-wide synergy, optimal or maximal relevant interpersonal encounter, realisation, and expression of transpersonal and transcendental potentialities, and related concepts, experiences and activities.[15]

And, as a playful aside to his far-reaching definition (which surely must rank as one of the earliest descriptions of what would later become the New Age) he added, 'How's that for a nice ride on "Astro-Bike" or perhaps better still, "Inner Space Bike"!'

Meanwhile, the correspondence between Sutich and Maslow continued. In November 1967 Maslow wrote suggesting that the word 'transpersonal' might be the best expression of all... 'The more I think of it', he noted, 'the more this word says what we are all trying to say, that is, beyond individuality, beyond the development of the individual person into something which is more inclusive than the individual person, or which is bigger than he is.'[16]

The term 'transpersonal' had first been used by Czechoslovakian psychiatrist Dr Stanislav Grof – later to be scholar-in-residence at Esalen Institute – during a lecture in Berkeley some two months earlier, and finally the expression carried the day. It was generally agreed that it was the most appropriate term for describing a psychology dedicated primarily to 'the advancement of mankind.'

There was now a sense that something really exciting was about to unfold – a new science dedicated to studying the real depths of human nature and hopefully providing a wonderful synthesis of knowledge relating to interpersonal relationships, self-realisation and transcendental potentialities.

As it transpired, the next decade would indeed see the full flowering of the Human Potential Movement, coinciding especially with the increasing influence of the Esalen Institute and the rapid development of personal growth centres around the United States. There could be no doubt about it, a new era was dawning.

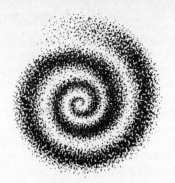

4 · ESALEN, GESTALT AND ENCOUNTER

North of San Simeon, the Californian coastline becomes increasingly craggy and precipitous. Highway 1 soon transforms into a narrow, winding courseway with spectacular cliff-edges falling away to the left and the sudden and dramatic Santa Lucia mountains rising up on the right. Wildflowers and lichen provide flashes of colour here and there, but much of the terrain is rugged and severe. However there are pockets of beautiful greenery as well – regal cypresses which grow in precarious positions, on impossible ledges, above sharp rock spurs which jut out from the crashing sea below.

Big Sur is only superficially tamed by man. Highway 1 was only completed in 1937 and even now is often blocked by falls of stone or pockets of fog which roll in from the ocean. It is also a route which dictates its own pace, for drivers who venture here do not speed along but wind carefully and humbly round the seemingly endless successions of hairpin bends, ever aware of the precarious balance between human life, cliff-edge and ocean.

The Spanish called this region after the river El Rio Grande de Sur, and the jagged, weaving coastline extends for some 80 kilometres, almost as far north as Carmel and Monterey. The town of Big Sur itself is still only a small settlement, famous mostly for its Nepenthe Inn, a vegetarian restaurant with impressive wooden sculptures and a wonderful view to the south. The controversial novelist, Henry Miller, also spent many years living near here as a recluse.

Esalen Institute is located between Big Sur township and the charming hamlet of Lucia. One comes upon it suddenly, and it too rests literally on the cliff-edge. A place of considerable natural beauty, it is now part of local folklore and has had much to do with the rise of the new consciousness.

Esalen Institute used to be known simply as Slate's Hot Springs. The land was acquired in 1910 by Henry Murphy, a doctor from Salinas, and he built the dwelling now known as the Big House, as a holiday home. By the late 1950s, however, the land had fallen into disrepair and Slate's Hot Springs was being visited mostly by Henry Miller and his circle of bohemian friends. Old Dr Murphy had long since died, the Big House was being maintained by a young macho writer named Hunter Thompson, and nothing much was happening except occasional brawls among the locals.

In 1962, however, things changed when Dr Murphy's son Michael and Zen Buddhism enthusiast Richard Price drove down to the property to have a new look at it. They came up with an idea that was to have far-reaching consequences – Big Sur Hot Springs, as it was now called, could be a meeting place for different spiritual traditions and for the exploration of consciousness. Philosophers, writers and mystics could come here to impart their knowledge and share their experiences. It could become a very special place indeed.

With this vision, the spirit of Esalen was born, although the Springs would still be known by their old name for three more years. The Lodge, a meeting room on the property up the hill from the Big House, became the centre for seminars, and early visitors associated with the Institute included Alan Watts, Aldous Huxley, Ken Kesey, Joan Baez, J.B. Rhine, Carlos Castaneda, Linus Pauling, Paul Tillich and, as we have already mentioned, Abraham Maslow.

By the latter half of the 1960s Esalen had extended its range of famous visitors to include Indian musician, Ali Akbar Khan, environmentalist, Buckminster Fuller and bodywork pioneer, Ida Rolf. Esalen soon acquired a reputation as an idyllic therapeutic hideaway: a place to enjoy weekend seminars and workshops, and discover your inner being. It was a place to get in touch with your feelings, awaken your senses, reach out to your partner, and enjoy the communal experience of bathing and massage on the cliff-edge above the Pacific Ocean.

Not everyone at Esalen was mystical, however, a notable exception being Fritz Perls, the distinguished founder of Gestalt Therapy. Arguably the most important single influence in the early years of Esalen, Perls took up residence there in a two-bedroom stone house built especially for him on the property. However he despised the 'woolly-headed' spiritual aspect of the personal growth movement and endeavoured to bring his own, much more confronting and sometimes brutal style of therapy to the fore.

While Gestalt Therapy was particular to Perls, Gestalt Psychology itself was much older – the movement dating back to a paper published by Max Wertheimer in 1912.

The German word *gestalt* refers to a pattern of parts making up a whole, and the underlying principle of Gestalt Psychology is that an analysis of parts does not lead to an understanding of the whole. Parts by themselves have no meaning. Building on the pioneering work of Wertheimer and also Wolfgang Kohler and Kurt Koffka, Perls noted that Gestalt theory applied to the personality and to basic human needs:

> Every organ, the senses, movements, thoughts, subordinate to [an] emerging need and are quick to change loyalty and function as soon as that need is satisfied and then retreat into the background. . . . All the parts of the organism identify themselves temporarily with the emergent gestalt.[1]

Born in Berlin in 1893, Perls had struggled through his youth and school years but went on to gain his MD in psychiatry. Then he moved to Vienna where he met Wilhelm Reich and returned to Germany in 1936 to deliver a paper at the Psychoanalytic Congress, attended by the founding father himself, Sigmund Freud.

Despite Freud's influence on his conceptual frameworks Perls came to the view quite early in his professional career that Freud's focus on sex and destructiveness as the twin motivating forces of human existence was incomplete. He rejected the idea of rigidly classifying instincts and analysing a patient's *past*, and chose to focus instead on the *here and now*. For people to be whole, or balanced, they needed to recognise bodily yearnings and impulses instead of disguising them. In fact, life was a series of gestalts that emerged one after the other – a variety of needs requiring satisfaction. Perls developed Gestalt Therapy to allow people to recognise their

Fritz Perls – father of Gestalt Therapy (Drawing Nevill Drury)

projections and disguises as real feelings and subsequently to be able to fulfil themselves.

After breaking with the Psychoanalytic movement, Fritz Perls emigrated to the United States in 1946 and established the New York Institute for Gestalt Therapy in 1952. He moved to California in 1959. His friend, fellow psychologist Wilson Van Dusen, explains how, at the time, Perls' views were revolutionary:

We were all basically retrospective, strongly retrospective, in both our analysis and therapies. We wouldn't conceive of understanding a patient without an extensive history. And for a man just to walk into a room and describe people's behaviour so accurately added a

43

whole new dimension. This is where I considered Fritz very great. His incomparable capacity to observe . . .[2]

Fritz Perls had been strongly influenced by Reich's idea that the body reflected internal psychological processes. The person *here and now* showed everything through his or her being and behaviour, there was no need to delve into analysis. 'Nothing is ever really repressed', he once commented, 'All relevant *gestalten* are emerging, they are on the surface, they are obvious like the emperor's nakedness . . .'[3]

As a therapist, Perls was often extremely curt and blunt, cutting through the niceties of social interaction to the person behind the image. At Esalen he would give demonstrations of Gestalt Therapy before over a hundred people. Sitting on a dais, he would invite members of the audience to participate with him in role-play. He had two chairs beside him. One was the so-called 'hot seat' which the participant sat in, engaging in dialogue with Perls. The other chair was there to help the person switch roles and enact different parts, engaging in the self-questioning process. Frequently volunteers revealed their weaknesses and limitations during these sessions but there was, after all, a lesson to be learnt.

Perls was very wary of the 'fun generation' who came to Esalen just for entertainment, and his dialogues with these people were always brutally honest. For some these were moments of revelation and awe, for others quite shattering experiences. Fritz Perls' publisher, Arthur Ceppos, recalls:

> I think that Fritz's greatest contribution was his horror at how ridiculous man permits himself to become; and by becoming aware of how ridiculous he is, he can emerge into an identity that is no longer ridiculous, but is relatively free. This is the whole secret behind Fritz's hot seat. He would show people how they made fools of themselves . . .[4]

Essentially Perls believed, with the Existentialists, that each person lived in his or her own universe and had to take the responsibility for their own behaviour and growth. The well-known Gestalt Therapy prayer, which was often displayed as a poster at this time, reads as follows:

> I do my thing, and you do your thing,
> I am not in this world to live up to your expectations
> And you are not in this world to live up to mine.
>   You are you and I am I,
> And if by chance we find each other, it's beautiful.
>   If not, it can't be helped.[5]

Tai Chi was popular at Esalen from the beginning

Self-awareness and honesty were crucial to Perls' concept of Gestalt Therapy: the essential point was to be aware of what you are experiencing, *how* you experience your existence *now*. Perls would urge people to pay particular attention to the ways in which they sabotaged their own attempts at sustained awareness, for these were ways in which they habitually prevented themselves from fully contacting the world and their own experiences.

Extending his scope from here-and-now interactions through dialogue and self-recognition, Perls also placed considerable emphasis on dreams. Here were messages that could help people understand the unfinished situations they were carrying around with them. In *Gestalt Therapy Verbatim* he wrote:

> In Gestalt Therapy we don't interpret dreams. We do something more interesting with them. Instead of analysing and further cutting up the dream, we want to bring it back to life. And the way to bring it back to life is to re-live the dream as if it were happening now. Instead of telling the dream as if it were a story in the past, act it out in the present, so that it becomes a part of yourself, so that you are really involved.[6]

Perls suggested dreams be written down with their various details as completely as possible. Then a dialogue or encounter between the different component parts or figures could be held. As the encounter process continued a new integration could be arrived at. Perls described the dream, in fact, as 'an excellent opportunity to find the holes in the personality . . . if you understand the meaning of each time you identify with some bit of a dream, each time you translate an *it* into an *I*, you increase in vitality and in your potential'.

At Esalen, although Perls worked alongside other notable figures like Bernard Gunther, who taught massage and sensory awakening, Gia-fu Feng who instructed in Tai Chi, and George Leonard, who held seminars on interracial issues, he was very much the 'star attraction' for a few years.

However, in the late 1960s a major rival emerged who would increasingly take much of the limelight – Will Schutz.

Schutz was a social psychologist who had graduated with a PhD from UCLA in 1951, worked at the University of Chicago, and later taught at Harvard and Berkeley. Like Perls, he too advocated a way of liberating people from their social conditioning and false self-images. However, whereas Perls relied mainly on acute personal observation and direct verbal interchange with his clients, Schutz used a method called Open Encounter and was building on an approach already developed by Carl Rogers and other American social scientists.

The concept of modern encounter therapy derives substantially from a training programme developed for community leaders in Connecticut in 1946. A feature of this programme was the regular feedback between trainers and participants, the idea being that such feedback would enhance the experience of all involved. Trainers from the Connecticut groups helped establish National Training Laboratories in 1947 to assist government and industry in assessing the efficiency of personnel. Basically NTL established a system of providing direct personal feedback through what became known as training groups, or T-groups. Schutz was thoroughly conversant with group therapy and the T-group approach when he arrived at Esalen in 1967.

In an encounter group there are usually between ten and fifteen people who sit in a circle on the floor. Often there is no specified leader. An encounter session may last for a few hours or extend into days and even weeks on end.

People taking part in an encounter group try to 'reach' and perceive each other in real ways and experience genuine inner feelings. Such therapy depends, of course, on developing honest relationships

Encounter groups – direct personal expression (Credit: Lew Luton)

with the others involved and expressing such feelings verbally or physically.

In the approach adopted by Carl Rogers, members of the encounter group would initially interact loosely, waiting for information on what to expect and how to act. A sense of frustration would often develop as the group came to realise that it had to determine its own direction. Often members would resist expressing themselves personally, but then ease out of this by beginning to discuss events and situations that occurred in the past.

Rogers discovered that it was quite common for the first encounter exchanges to be negative ('I don't find you appeal to me'; 'Your manner of talking irritates me'; 'You are very superficial') but this was because deep positive feelings were harder to express than negative sentiments. Usually, however, providing the group passed through this phase without fragmenting, personally meaningful material would begin to come through and a sense of trust would emerge. As sensitive and important recollections rose to the surface, the members of the group would begin to respond by seeking to help other members of the group who had deep inner problems.

It was this type of orientation that Schutz brought to Esalen. An admirer of Rogers, his particular emphasis in group therapy was to help people feel good about themselves. In fact, Schutz published a best-selling book titled *Joy: Expanding Human Awareness*, soon after his arrival at Esalen. In it, he explained that the attainment of joy was at the very core of his approach:

> Joy is the feeling that comes from the fulfilment of one's potential. Fulfilment brings to an individual the feeling that he can cope with his environment; the sense of confidence in himself as a significant, competent, lovable person who is capable of handling situations as they arise, able to use fully his own capacities, and free to express his feelings.[7]

Initially Perls welcomed Schutz's presence at Esalen. He seemed to have solid academic credentials and was not a dreamy mystic like so many other visitors to the Institute. Perls may also have thought of Schutz as a potential convert to Gestalt Therapy. But it soon became clear that Schutz was intent on being his own person and developing his own reputation. His book brought considerable publicity to Esalen and when *Time* magazine published a largely favourable article on Esalen in 1967, ironically there was no mention of either Perls or Gestalt Therapy. Not surprisingly, Perls' nose was somewhat 'put out-of-joint'. The slightly embittered Gestalt therapist now began describing Schutz's Open Encounter sessions as insubstantial distractions – good fun perhaps, but not to be taken seriously. A sense of resentment was beginning to take hold.

Nevertheless, Schutz continued to hold increasingly successful seminars at Esalen although he had critics apart from Fritz Perls. Some mainstream psychotherapists elsewhere in the country maintained that it was unwise to encourage the sort of encounter sessions Schutz was holding, because there was no scope for further follow-up: the therapist in charge could hardly assume responsibility for what might happen to participants later on. Schutz responded to this by emphasising that you could do whatever you were willing to take responsibility for, and that included any clients wishing to involve themselves in encounter therapy. Obviously, Open Encounter was potentially a risk-taking exercise, since there was always the possibility that hurtful or damaging material could be uncovered. However Schutz also pointed out that Esalen was essentially for people who were healthy, its main aim being to help already comparatively well-balanced individuals with their self-actualisation process, rather than providing care for people who were mentally ill. In the final analysis, said Schutz, everyone coming to Esalen had to take the responsibility for what they experienced there. It was up to them to respond to the challenge of self-transformation.

During the later 1960s the range of seminars offered at Esalen expanded rapidly – from some twenty programme options in 1965 to around 120 in 1968. However, the exciting expansion of activities at Esalen was not without its human casualties, and part of the problem was related to casual experimentation with mind-altering drugs.

The attitude to psychedelics at Esalen in the early years had always been comparatively relaxed – Alan Watts had described his aesthetic and mystical experiences with psilocybin and LSD in his 1962 publication *The Joyous Cosmology* and Aldous Huxley, who, like Watts, was an early visitor to Big Sur, had related his wondrous encounter with mescalin in *The Doors of Perception*. Michael Murphy had himself experimented with peyote buttons in the Big House at Esalen in the early 1960s and Carlos Castaneda explained the shamanic use of psychedelics during a celebrated visit to Esalen around the same time.

However, the psychedelic experience *per se* was not advocated at Esalen. Seminars on the relationship between drugs and mystical and religious experiences were held there from time to time but they were intended as theoretical seminars, not experiential workshops. It soon became necessary to include in Esalen brochures a note to the effect that no drugs would be used in such sessions.

Nevertheless, the first death associated with Esalen was drug-related. Lois Delattre was a member of the first residential programme at Esalen and later went to work in Esalen's San Francisco office. Like many others in the personal growth movement at that time she had experimented with LSD, but she also wanted to explore the effects of the so-called 'love drug', MDA, an amphetamine derivative of iso-saffrole which heightened sensory awareness and was said to produce states of emotional openness. Delattre succeeded in locating some MDA and took it with three other friends. However she soon became very introspective and left to lie down on a bed. For a while she seemed to be breathing deeply, as if in a trance, but when her companions later returned they found her dead.

Delattre's death caused a distinct sense of panic at Esalen. Even though it was not directly attributable to an Institute programme it did highlight what no-one had yet seriously considered – that the quest for new realms of consciousness could result in a fatality.

The next deaths at Esalen were not drug-related but they too had a strong impact on the Esalen community. Marcia Price had attended Fritz Perls' Gestalt Therapy workshops and was employed in the Esalen office. She was also sexually involved with Perls, who had acquired a well-earned reputation as a womaniser. The news that Marcia Price had committed suicide by shooting herself devastated members of the Residential Programme at Esalen and had a profoundly sobering effect on everyone who knew her. It was later revealed that Fritz Perls had mocked her suicide threats during a Gestalt Therapy session.

Then, to exacerbate matters still further, a young woman named Judith Gold drowned herself in the Esalen baths, early in 1969. Gold, too, had experienced a traumatic encounter with Perls; she had similarly threatened suicide while sitting in his 'hot seat' and had been savagely jeered by Perls in response.

Perls himself was not especially compassionate or conciliatory after these deaths, maintaining that people who were potential suicide cases should be treated just like anyone else. If you were threatening to kill yourself, Perls would tell you to go right ahead and do it. However, the mood at Esalen changed dramatically after these unfortunate incidents, and Perls' relationship with Michael Murphy began to sour. Perls in turn became increasingly disturbed by the escalating street violence in California and also felt that the political ascendancy of Ronald Reagan as Governor of California and the resurgence of George Wallace and Richard Nixon heralded a new right-wing direction in the United States which reminded him of events in Nazi Germany. With these factors welling up in his mind, and colleagues on all sides accusing him of paranoia, Perls decided to leave Esalen in 1969 and establish himself instead in Canada, where he had a number of students. Perls purchased a motel alongside Lake Cowichan on Vancouver Island, naming it the Gestalt Institute of British Columbia, but did not live to see its development. He died six months after founding it, in March 1970.

The dramatic years of Fritz Perls at Esalen were undoubtedly a potent lesson for the Human Potential Movement and provided ample demonstration that the brutal stripping away of personal defence mechanisms could, in some instances, have tragic consequences. At the end of it all, Will Schutz's more optimistic mode of encounter therapy seemed more compatible with the Esalen style, and he outlasted Fritz Perls by several years. Schutz continued his Open Encounter sessions at the Institute until 1973, before deciding to leave and head north to San Francisco.

Today the range of experiential workshops offered at Esalen is enormous. People come to learn techniques of Tai Chi, massage, Zen, hypnosis, dance, shamanism, Taoism, 'Creative Sexuality' and Feldenkrais body awareness, or to attend lectures on the new physics, Gnosticism, Findhorn or feminist religions. The range is diverse and ever-changing, but Esalen is also much less controversial than it used to be. The general public now has a greater familiarity with mysticism, the various mind and body therapies, and the notion of 'health for the whole person'.

However, it took some time for these holistic frameworks to emerge. In the late 1960s the full impact of the psychedelic era was still to be felt, and there would be important implications here for the Human Potential Movement and the exploration of altered states of consciousness.

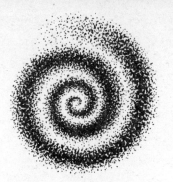

5 · The Psychedelic Years

For many people the psychedelic era is epitomised by the so-called 'Summer of Love' in 1966–7, which shrouded San Francisco's Haight–Ashbury district in a haze of drug-induced joy-consciousness. It was at this time that the media first began to draw attention to the emergent counter-culture, that rapidly increasing body of youth who were rebelling against the materialism of the 'American Dream', against the hostilities perpetrated upon the gentle people of South Vietnam, and in response to the rising levels of violence in cities at home.

The psychedelic generation was characterised by hippies espousing a message of peace and wearing flowers in their hair. The hippies themselves were mostly young people who felt themselves outside mainstream society, alienated from its values, and determined to overthrow cultural norms with displays of bizarre behaviour. So it was a time, too, of hand-painted, multi-coloured Volkswagen vans, exotic and unconventional clothes, patchouli incense, itinerant folk-singers and innovative rock groups like The Grateful Dead, Jefferson Airplane, Quicksilver Messenger Service and Big Brother and the Holding Company. It was also a time of widespread recreational

A psychedelic drawing by Lee Conklin, published by The Print Mint (Credit: *The Psychedelic Review*)

drug use. LSD was readily available to 'acid trippers' in such forms as White Lightning or Orange Sunshine; marijuana was commonplace and smoked openly in the streets; and 'hash cookies' were favourite fare at parties. Somewhat after the fashion of Fritz Perls, who was proclaiming a similar message at Esalen, street banners urged a message of personal liberation. One characteristic poster announced: 'The time has come to be free. BE FREE. Do your thing. Be what you are. Do it. NOW.'[1]

The Psychedelic Shop, run by Jay and Ron Thelin, opened at 1535 Haight Street, San Francisco, on New Year's Day 1966. It sold all manner of books, records and psychedelic posters while also reserving a third of its floor space for a 'calm centre', where hippies could come to meditate or sleep. Down the road were eateries like Tracy's and the psychedelically decorated Drogstore Cafe, while The Print Mint sold old movie posters, served as a community centre where people could leave messages for each other, and was invariably inhabited by wandering musicians and appreciative hippies. The Haight–Ashbury, or Hashbury, district was also served by a newspaper called *The Oracle*, which was hawked in the streets and distributed through various 'alternative' outlets around the Haight. Printed in different coloured inks, which tended to fuse together in rainbow patterns, *The Oracle* kept residents up-to-date with what was happening in the local community, as well as publishing controversial articles on such diverse topics as the horrors of prisoner-of-war camps and the joys of masturbation. Joyce Ann Francisco, who sold advertising for *The Oracle*, told *Time* reporter Judson Gooding that she loved being a hippie. 'Human beings need total freedom', she said enthusiastically, 'That's where God is at. We need to shed hypocrisy, dishonesty, phoniness, and go back to the purity of our childhood values.' She also epitomised the casual, hedonistic approach to drugs in the Haight–Ashbury subculture. 'Whatever turns me on is a sacrament – LSD, sex, my bells, my colours. This is the holy communion. . . . When I find myself becoming confused, I drop out and take a dose of acid. It's a short-cut to reality – throws you right into it. . .'[2]

The Haight, of course, had its own pantheon of heroes. For example, there was novelist Richard Brautigan, who would later become fashionable as the acclaimed author of such novels as *Trout Fishing in America* and *In Watermelon Sugar*. He would parade in the streets carrying a mirror and calling out to surprised visitors and tourists, 'Know thyself!' Also a feature of the local scene were such figures as psychedelic artist Michael Bowen, who would later help create the Love Pageant Rally; The Diggers, who would feed hundreds of hungry passers-by free of charge at The Panhandle; poets Allen Ginsberg and Michael McClure; lead singer with the The Grateful Dead, Jerry Garcia, and poster artists Stanley Mouse, Alton Kelley and Wilfried Satty. Local entrepreneur Bill Graham staged many of the early acid-rock concerts at San Francisco's Fillmore Auditorium – including performances by Janis Joplin and Grace Slick – so that made him a special figure in the counter-culture, and there were dramatic impromptu street theatre performances by the Mime Troupe who were dedicated, as they said themselves, to 'undermining society'. Meanwhile LSD biochemist August Owsley Stanley III was famous for producing the best 'acid' in the country, and hippie poetess Lenore Kandel became notorious overnight for her collection of rapturous, sexually explicit poems, *The Love Book*.

It was a crazy, happy, somewhat reckless time and for a while it must have seemed that it could go on forever. But then came an announcement that on 6 October 1966 the State of California would ban the use of LSD, a date which some associated with the symbolism of 666, the mark of the Beast. However, if the people's sacrament was about to be taken away, a response was soon forthcoming. Michael Bowen and the Psychedelic Rangers declared that on the same day as the banning there would be a Love Pageant Rally at Panhandle Park between Masonic Avenue and Ashbury Street. The 'protest' invitation sent by the Rangers to Mayor John F. Shelley also provided a clear indication of the schism which was now rapidly building between the psychedelic generation and 'straight' society:

Sir,

Opposition to an unjust law creates futility for citizens who are its victims and increases the hostility between the governed and the governors. In the case of the LSD prohibition, the State has entered directly into the sacrosanct, personal psyches of its citizens. Our Love Pageant Rally is intended to overcome the paranoia and separation with which the State wishes to divide and silence the increasing revolutionary sense of Californians. Similar rallies will be held in communities such as ours all over the country and in Europe. You are invited to attend and address our rally. Thankyou.

Sincerely yours,

Citizens for the Love Pageant Rally of
October 6, 1966[3]

The rally began, as promised, on the morning of 6 October, as employees of *The Oracle* and the Psychedelic Shop led a delegation to City Hall, laden with flowers and morning glory seeds and intent on 'turning on' Mayor Shelley. Later, as crowds steadily gathered, an impromptu stage was created on the back of a truck for The Grateful Dead, Janis Joplin and Big Brother and the Holding Company, and the rally burst into full flight. It was a joyous time, 'a hell of a gathering', with three thousand people really enjoying themselves. One observer was moved to say: 'It's just being. Humans *being*. Being together. . .' 'Yes', agreed Michael Bowen, 'It's a Human Be-In.'

In such a way, the term 'Be-In' came into use as part of the popular street culture of the time. But Bowen didn't want things to stop there, now that they were gathering momentum. After meeting with Allen Cohen, editor of *The Oracle*, it was agreed that there should be a much bigger love-rally in San Francisco, a rally which would be remembered for years to come.

The date planned was 14 January 1967, in the afternoon. There would be a 'Gathering of the Tribes for a Human Be-In at the Polo Fields in Golden Gate Park'. In a press-release issued two days prior to the event it was announced that:

> Berkeley political activists and the love generation of the Haight–Ashbury will join together with members of the new nation who will be coming from every state in the nation, every tribe of the young (the emerging soul of the nation) to powwow, celebrate and prophesy the epoch of liberation, love, peace, compassion and unity of mankind. The night of bruited fear of the American eagle-breast-body is over. Hang your fear at the door and join the future. If you do not believe, please wipe your eyes and see.[4]

Another press-release provided more specific details of what one could expect:

> Twenty to fifty thousand people are expected to gather for a joyful powwow and Peace Dance to be celebrated with leaders, guides and heroes of our generation. Timothy Leary will make his first Bay Area Public appearance; Allen Ginsberg will chant and read with Gary Snyder, Michael McClure and Lenore Kandel; Dick Alpert, Jerry Rubin, Dick Gregory and Jack Weinberg will speak. Music will be played by all the Bay Area rock bands, including The Grateful Dead, Big Brother, and the Holding Company, Quicksilver Messenger Service, and many others.

Everyone is invited to bring costumes, blankets, bells, flags, symbols,
cymbals, drums, beads, feathers, flowers.[5]

This time around 10,000 people would attend in a union of love and
activism. It was clearly an auspicious day, for as astrologer Ambrose
Hollingsworth had calculated, it marked the time when the present
population of the earth would be equal in number to the total
number of dead in the whole of human history. Obviously, some
positive demonstration of human communication was called for on
this special occasion.

Luckily 14 January was a crisp winter day, the sun beaming down
as thousands of hippies mingled together, waving their colourful
banners, burning incense, smoking marijuana, sharing food, and
carrying flowers. There were giggling children, frolicking animals,
Hare Krishnas beating on drums, and a procession of guest speakers
and musicians. Jefferson Airplane and Quicksilver Messenger Service played their rock songs before an enthusiastic audience, Allen
Ginsberg chanted 'We are one! We are all one!' and Timothy Leary
declared 'Whatever you do is beautiful. . .'. Near the grandstands a
group of whites and negroes played guitars and flutes together, and a
few members of the famous Hell's Angels motorcycle gang also came
to watch, clad in black-leather sleeveless jackets. They too mingled
amidst the incense and the flowers. Amazingly, there were no fights
and the crowd was extraordinarily well behaved all afternoon. As
the sun set across the park there was a profound feeling of deep and
pervasive peace.

The gathering was acclaimed by all who had participated as a great
success and afterwards Michael Bowen and Allen Ginsberg were
ecstatic – it was the birth of a new era, and a new-found harmony
of consciousness. For others it even seemed like Eden regained, lost
innocence rediscovered. But the question on everyone's lips was:
Would it last? Would the Summer of Love simply prove ephemeral?
Would the joy-consciousness endure? Would psychedelics transform
the nation?

As it turned out, the hippie phenomenon of Haight–Ashbury would
not last very long at all. Within a year the Psychedelic Shop had
closed down, Michael Bowen moved to Mexico to paint, The Oracle's
Allen Cohen moved to Northern California to write, and there was a
general dispersal of local energy.

However, it would be a mistake to identify the impact of 'hippie
consciousness' simply with what happened during the Summer
of Love in San Francisco. In many ways this manifestation of

psychedelic culture was simply the most visible expression of a much wider phenomenon which had now begun to filter across the whole country. There were hippies all over the United States -- in Boston, Seattle, Detroit, New Orleans, Austin, and New York. In June 1967 a gathering of hippies met in Greenwich Village's Washington Square Park to assist the cause of dog owners protesting against the leash laws. Here, revelling in playful paradox, they chanted 'What is dog spelled backwards?' And in Stone Place Mall in Dallas, around a hundred 'flower children' assembled to protest against an ordinance intended to ban large public gatherings. There were also small hippie communities springing up around the country, like the group who lived at 'Drop City' near Trinidad, Colorado, in a cluster of geodesic domes constructed from old automobile tops, and the hippies at Morning Star Ranch near Sebastopol, north of San Francisco.

But the actual issue of psychedelic consciousness – the relationship of mind-altering drugs to perception and their role in the personal quest for transcendence – had arisen many years prior to the Summer of Love. As indicated earlier, the subject of psychedelics was of considerable interest during the early years of Esalen, and had featured in the writings of Aldous Huxley and Alan Watts. And there were other figures, too, in this debate. They included a group of psychologists who worked at Harvard University and who had already attracted national attention for their views on psychedelic and personal transformation.

Ralph Metzner, Richard Alpert and Timothy Leary all had distinguished academic backgrounds. German-born Metzner had graduated from Oxford University in 1958 and received a doctorate in clinical psychology from Harvard University in 1962. The following year he became a post-doctoral fellow, specialising in psychopharmacology, at Harvard Medical School.

Richard Alpert – later to be known to the world as Baba Ram Dass – had taken his doctorate at Stanford University and in 1953 became an assistant professor at Harvard University. In 1956 he was appointed co-director of the Harvard Psychedelic Drug Research Project. And Timothy Leary, who would become famous and notorious for his psychedelic dictum 'Turn On, Tune In and Drop Out', had a similarly impeccable academic background. After gaining a Masters degree at Washington State University in 1946 he earned his PhD from the University of California in 1950 for his thesis 'The Social Dimensions of Personality'. He published a conventional textbook, *The Interpersonal Diagnosis of Personality* in 1957 and was appointed to the Harvard Center for Personality Research in 1960. As it transpired, this triumvirate of PhDs, Metzner, Alpert and Leary, would become pioneers of the psychedelic revolution.

During the summer vacation in the first year of his new position at Harvard, Leary took his two children down to Cuernavaca in Mexico. As Leary writes in his autobiography, *Flashbacks*, 'In the days of Montezuma this town, called "horn-of-the-cow", was the home of soothsayers, wise men and magicians. Cuernavaca lies south of a line of volcanic peaks, Popo, Ixtacihuatl, and Toluca. On the slopes of the volcanoes grow the sacred mushrooms of Mexico, divinatory fungi, *teonanacatl*, flesh of the gods.'[6] It would be his encounter with the flesh of the gods that would transform his perspective.

In their holiday villa the Learys had several guests call on them, including Gerhart Braun, an anthropologist from the University of Mexico. Braun had studied Aztec culture, had translated various Nahuatl texts, and was intrigued by the references he had found in their literature to sacred mushrooms, known locally as *hongos*. Leary asked if he could perhaps locate some. A week later Braun phoned to say that he had obtained several such mushrooms from a *curandera*, or folk healer, in the village of San Pedro near Toluca, and perhaps they should try them. Braun came round with some friends, spread the mushrooms out in two bowls, and said to Leary that everyone should take six. It was generally agreed that they tasted a lot worse than they looked, but expectations were high.

The *hongos* made Leary slightly nauseous at first, and his face began to tingle. Soon his vision was awash with wafty hallucinatory impressions, and like Aldous Huxley who had charted this strange terrain before him, he began to discover a profound richness in the kaleidoscopic imagery unfolding before his eyes:

Mosaics flaming colour Muzo emerald, Burma Rubies
Ceylon Sapphire,
Mosaics lighted from within, glowing, moving, changing,
Hundred reptiles, jewel encrusted. . .[7]

He now began to ponder the nature of his own life-force, his bloodstream, his pulsing arteries. The organic basis of all creativity overwhelmed him. His body contained a myriad universes; his cell tissue seemed to hold the secret of life and energy.

Leary was perceiving the motions of the universe at the atomic and subatomic levels. Finite imagery had been left far behind. He was witnessing the tides and motions of energy and form in their most profoundly elementary and essential phases of manifestation.

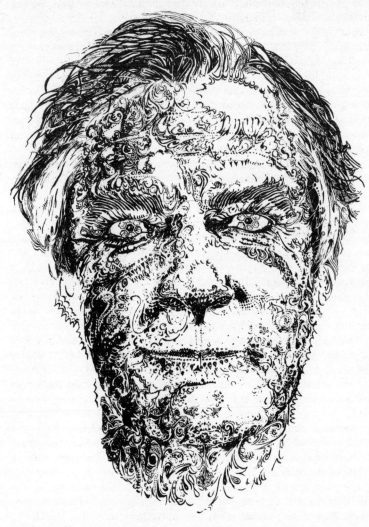

Timothy Leary – 'You are never the same after you have had the veil drawn'
(Credit: Michael Green/*The Psychedelic Review*)

And surprising though it must have seemed, the experience was quintessentially *religious*: 'I came back a changed man. You are never the same after you have had that one flash glimpse down the cellular time tunnel. You are never the same after you have had the veil drawn.'[8]

It was this initiatory experience which led Leary and his friends towards a systematic exploration of inner space. It seemed to him that a new chapter in the development of human thought was beginning: the quest for greater consciousness. There had been visionaries before, but they had all been isolated individuals. Now a *movement* could get underway. The earlier mystics and seers were forerunners and could act as guides:

> We did sense that we were not alone. The quest for internal freedom, for the elixir of life, for the draught of immortal revelation was not new. We were part of an ancient and honorable fellowship which had pursued this journey since the dawn of recorded history. We began to read the accounts of early trippers – Dante, Hesse, Rene Daumal, Tolkien, Homer, Blake, George Fox, Swedenborg, Bosch, and the explorers from the Orient – Tantrics, Sufis, Bauls, Gnostics, Hermetics, Sivits, Saddhus. . . no, we were not alone.[9]

During the autumn and winter of 1960, Leary spent most of his spare time studying the hallucinogenic qualities of psychotropic mushrooms. By day he continued to deliver lectures on clinical psychology at the Harvard Graduate School.

One of his students, a man who seemed to Leary at the time to be rather academic and 'ivory towerish' in his attitudes, but nevertheless brilliant at his work, was Ralph Metzner. Metzner said he wanted to experiment with psilocybin – a psychedelic synthesised from the mushroom *Psilocybe mexicana* – and was keen to evaluate its impact on prison inmates. He thought that it could provide them with an experience which would change the pattern of their lives. Of course there was no way in which they could predict the outcome, or the reaction of either inmates or wardens, but perhaps it could lead to new methods of integration and rehabilitation.

And so began a series of psychedelic prison sessions. At first they weren't entirely successful. Leary on one occasion found himself viewing one of the inmates, a Polish embezzler, with acute distrust. Someone put on a jazz record, alleviating the tension, and everyone relaxed. However the mood ebbed and flowed. As Leary later recalled: 'There were high points and low points, ecstasies and terror.'

61

There were more sessions. Some of the convicts were able to leave on parole. Mild-mannered and changed men, they were sometimes, on Leary's admission, unable to cope with society's pressures. However, the prison, and its psychiatric unit had become, in certain measure, a 'spiritual centre'. It was a step towards a new understanding.

The prison sessions inspired Leary towards a sense of brotherhood. He had found communication, albeit uneasy, with men of quite a different ilk from him. The psilocybin had unshackled the psychiatric doctor–inmate–warden roles and they were 'all men at one. . . all two-billion year-old seed centres pulsing together'. But the effect was not enduring. 'As time slowly froze' noted Leary, 'we were reborn in the old costumes and picked up the tired games. We weren't yet ready to act on our revelation.'

It took an eccentric Englishman, Michael Hollingshead, to point out the next stage along the way. Hollingshead was a writer-cum-yoga practitioner who devised plots for his novels with a semi-autobiographical basis. He also had a strong interest in psychedelics. Furthermore he had taken LSD, the most potent of all hallucinogens in terms of dose and quantity, and he urged Leary to do so. At first Leary refrained. LSD was a chemical, synthesised in a laboratory, whereas the mushrooms had natural and even a cultural basis. They grew in the ground; the Aztecs regarded them as holy.

Hollingshead insisted that LSD was of overwhelming 'religious' significance, paling the mushrooms by comparison. Leary was eventually won over. Together with a group of friends, he and Hollingshead consumed a dose in November 1961. Once again he found himself falling into an eddy of transforming shapes and forms. On reflection he thought of his role as father of his children. Had he been living a sham existence based merely on a routine form of parental devotion? Suddenly he seemed to be surrounded with death and falsity. Amid the confusion, what could be said to be *real*? He considered the structures and patterns of society: cultivation of crops, cities, invasions, migrations, moral codes, laws – but eventually these too seemed illusory as a basis for *being*. They were merely constructs and episodes of man; they did not identify his origins.

Leary now found himself falling inwards, beyond structure, into energy: '. . . nothing existed except whirring vibrations, and each illusory form was simply a different frequency'. His perception seemed reduced to a primal level, but then, as the effects began to wear off, he experienced a terrible sense of loss. He had been to the heart of an energy vortex. 'Why had we lost it?' he asked. 'Why were we being reborn?. . . in these silly leather bodies with these trivial little cheese-board minds?'

Leary had reached a level of consciousness which for the first time had seemed to define a sense of reality and being-ness. He had never reached this level before. He had never been to the core. Why couldn't it be more accessible?

Meanwhile he continued to explore other hallucinogens as a means of entry to these states of realisation. He partook of DMT with his colleague Richard Alpert, and discussed these experiences with Alan Watts, and also with William Burroughs, who had chronicled in some detail the effects of *yage* in the South American jungle. He began to ponder whether the visions of the mystics and seers of the past had a biochemical origin. Was he entering the same 'psychic spaces' as Jacob Boehme, William Blake and St John of the Cross had before him? Leary meanwhile received some inkling about these matters from an unexpected source.

As with the prison experiments suggested by Ralph Metzner, the new development similarly owed its impetus to the enthusiasm of a Harvard student. This time it was Walter Pahnke, young and eager, with a medical degree and a divinity qualification already under his belt and currently undertaking PhD studies in the philosophy of religion. Pahnke wanted to pin down the visionary experience within experimental parameters. Twenty theological students could be assembled in a church setting. Some would be given psilocybin while others would remain as the 'control group'. There would be organ music, prayers and a sermon – all the normal things in a Protestant service – and it would be interesting to see whether anyone found themselves expanding their consciousness in a transcendental, mystical direction.

Leary thought Pahnke's suggestion was outrageous, but the student insisted. He had a medical degree, after all, and would undertake psychiatric interviews to screen out 'pre-psychotics' beforehand. The volunteers would be carefully chosen and the experiment would proceed in the respectable presence of Dr Walter Huston Clark, a visiting theological scholar, and Dean Howard Thurman of the Boston University Chapel.

Pahnke was using as his framework a list of common mystical attributes that had been drawn up by W. T. Stace, a leading scholar in the field of comparative religion. These attributes, or qualities, fell under nine headings which represented the most commonly reported aspects of mystical experience, and are as follows.

Unity Both within and without in the external world. A profound sense of 'one-ness'.

Transcendence of time and space The mystical experience is not contained within three-dimensional space. It is often described as 'eternal' and 'infinite'.

Deeply felt positive mood Joy, blessedness and peace impart to the person the sense that his experience has been of incalculable value.

The sense of sacredness Something is beheld which has the quality of being able to be profaned. There is a profound sense of awe.

Objectivity and reality Knowledge and illumination: the experience seems to be overwhelmingly authoritative. No 'proof' is necessary – 'ultimate reality carries its own sense of certainty'.

Paradoxicality Rational interpretations following the illumination seem to be logically contradictory. An all-encompassing unity devoid of specific attributes is also in another sense an emptiness, and so on.

Alleged ineffability Words fail to express adequately the mystical experience.

Transiency Mystical consciousness is not sustained indefinitely; it is more of a 'peak experience'.

Persisting positive changes in attitude and behaviour Lasting psychological changes are experienced which affect the quality of interaction with others, and with life itself. The mystical experience itself is held in awe, and one is more at peace with oneself.

Known eventually as the 'Good Friday Experiment', Pahnke's session took place, as planned, on Good Friday 1962 in the chapel at Boston University. Ten of the theological students were given psilocybin while the others were given nicotinic acid, a vitamin which causes transient feelings of warmth and tingling in the skin. The participants listened to a 2½-hour religious service consisting of organ music, four solos, readings, prayers and personal meditation. During the weeks before the experiment, special care had been taken to reduce fear and maximise expectancy, and during the session participants did not know whether they had taken the psilocybin or the placebo.

Pahnke collected data for up to six months afterwards, and each student had prepared by this time an account of his own personal experiences. The following are Pahnke's statistics, which condensed as percentages are admittedly clinical. They do, however, make interesting reading.

Of those who had taken psilocybin, 70 per cent experienced *inner* unity, and 38 per cent *external*. 84 per cent had a sense of transcendence of time and space, 57 per cent other positive mood, 53 per cent a feeling of sacredness, 63 per cent the sense of objectivity and reality, 61 per cent the element of paradoxicality, 66 per cent ineffability, 79 per cent transiency, and an average of 50 per cent were substantially changed in psychological attitudes, along the lines of Stace's framework.

The control group, that is to say, those who had taken nicotinic acid, for the most part had much less intense religious experiences. The most pronounced sentiment was the feeling of love (positive mood) which was felt by 33 per cent. Otherwise the figures were: unity (7 per cent); time and space (6 per cent); positive mood (23 per cent); sacredness (28 per cent); objectivity and reality (18 per cent); paradoxicality (13 per cent); ineffability (18 per cent); transiency (8 per cent) and psychological changes (8 per cent).

Pahnke's experiment did not in itself offer proof that a person partaking of psychedelic substances would necessarily have a mystical experience, and it is clear that this is not the case. However the session did seem to show the value of hallucinogens in intensifying what would normally be a mild and rare religious experience. Within a religious setting it was therefore not surprising that any expansion of consciousness would be in a mystical direction.

The Good Friday Experiment had an impact on Leary's concept that set (mental attitude) and setting (the chosen supportive environment) were important factors in the outcome of a psychedelic session and he subsequently wrote, 'Our studies, naturalistic and experimental ...demonstrate that if the expectation, preparation and setting are spiritual, an intense mystical or revelatory experience can be expected in from 40 to 90 per cent of subjects.'[10]

When man ascends to the lofty heights of spiritual consciousness during a mystical illumination, his personality undergoes transformation. His new vision allows him to see the limitations of his ego-based human frameworks – his jealousies, fears, guilt, insecurities and so on – as if from a new, more far-reaching vantage point. On his return, if he is able, he will bring some of his unifying spiritual knowledge back into normal consciousness, assimilating it and hopefully remoulding the earlier and more limited personality which existed prior to the mystical experience.

It is meaningful, therefore, to speak of mystical consciousness as a type of *rebirth*. Not only does one change, but the more negative, or non-integrated, aspects of one's being are subsumed in favour of a more positive, integrated perspective.

Leary, Metzner and Alpert were intrigued by the transformative potential of the psychedelics but they now began to wonder if they should develop or incorporate some sort of guiding framework for their mystical ventures. The East is the direction of new light by day and it was perhaps appropriate that Leary and his colleagues sought a Buddhist framework for their drug-oriented mystical orientation. They clearly needed a well-charted basis for structuring the ego-death and spiritual-rebirth sequence on the psychedelic journey, and this framework would be the basis of a manual they would write together, *The Psychedelic Experience*.

They chose as their model the *Bardo Thodol* or *Tibetan Book of the Dead*, which had been translated into English by W.Y. Evans-Wentz. Aldous Huxley, who was also a practising Buddhist, had prized this Mahayana text and had alluded to it in *The Doors of Perception*.

Leary stressed that the *Bardo Thodol* was really addressed to the living, those who had necessarily to face the inevitability of death. On the one hand a sequence of post-mortem visions was described: the successive *Bardo* phases of consciousness in between separate incarnations. Leary noted, however, that these descriptions were in fact an esoteric guide to mind-expansion as well as a manual from which Tibetan priests read to those near death. The *Bardo* levels were realms of consciousness with which one could familiarise oneself prior to the final post-mortem separation of mind and body.

The *Bardo Thodol* begins with the loftiest experience of all: the Clear Light of Illumination experienced as the beholder loses his own ego in favour of the Void. This is a state of transcendent equilibrium and knowledge, of well-being and Unity with All. It is a state of sublime Liberation from the constrictions of the sensory world.

If this state of being cannot be maintained, there dawns the Secondary Clear Light. This occurs at a primal mystical level where the beholder is illuminated in an ecstasy which Leary called *wave energy flow*: 'The individual becomes aware that he is part of and surrounded by a charged field of energy, which seems almost electrical.' If he rides with the flow he may sustain this level of consciousness. However, should he attempt to control it, this in itself would indicate an act of *ego*, in turn reflective of *duality* – the sense of oneself distinct from the surroundings. The flow of energy associated with the experience of Unity and the heights of Kundalini would then ebb away and the individual would begin to fall into lower levels of mind referred to in the *Bardo Thodol* as the *Chonyid Bardo*, or karmic hallucinatory stages.

In the second *Bardo*, wrote Leary,

> strange sounds, weird sights and disturbed visions may occur. These can awe, frighten and terrify unless one is prepared. . . any and every shape – human, divine, diabolic, heroic, evil, animal, thing – which the human brain conjured up or the past life recalls, can present itself to consciousness; shapes and forms and sounds whirling by endlessly. The underlying solution – repeated again and again – is to recognise that your brain is producing the visions. They do not exist. Nothing exists except as your consciousness gives it life.

It was in this phase that the Tibetans believed they would encounter the Seven Peaceful Deities and the Seven Visions of the Wrathful Deities – their own counterpart of the Western Heaven and Hell. These deities incorporated fifty-eight embodiments of the human personality couched within traditional, culturally delineated forms and together with lower grades of potencies and forces constituted the Tibetan pantheon as a whole. Evans-Wentz described these deities as follows:

> The chief deities themselves are the embodiments of universal divine forces, with which the deceased is inseparably related, for through him, as being the microcosm of the macrocosm, penetrate all impulses and forces, good and bad alike. Samanta-Bhadra, the All-Good, thus personifies Reality, the Primordial Clear Light of the Unborn, Unshaped *Dharma-Kaya*. Vairochana is the Originator of all phenomena, the Cause of all Causes. As the Universal Father, Vairochana manifests or spreads forth as seed, or semen, all things; his *shakti*, the Mother of Great Space, is the Universal Womb into which the seed falls and evolves as the world systems. Vajra-Sattva symbolises Immutability. Ratna-Sambhava is the Beautifier, the Source of all Beauty in the Universe. Amitabha is Infinite Compassion and Love Divine, the *Christos*.

Amogha-Siddhi is the personification of Almighty Power or Omnipotence. And the minor deities, heroes, *dakinis* (or 'fairies'), goddesses, lords of death, *rakshasas*, demons, spirits and all others, correspond to definite human thoughts, passions and impulses, high and low, human and sub-human and super-human, in *karmic* form, as they take shape from the seeds of thought forming in the percipient's consciousness-content.[11]

In the *Bardo Thodol* the third phase, or *Sidpa Bardo*, is the period of 're-entry', the descent from the heights of the Here and Now to the familiar everyday environment. According to Mahayana tradition, a person able to bring full knowledge of spiritual unity down to his temporal existence would be an avatar, or saint. Below this level there would be various levels of inspirational attainment ranging from greater-than-normal human perception right down to the lowest forms of animal consciousness re-awakened in man.

In the *Bardo* teachings, since the dimensions of mind which the beholder experiences are directly related to his ability to retain control over thought and not be 'captured' by its imagery, it is important that during the 're-entry', the will should be focused as much as possible on integrated spiritual values rather than symbols of the ego. Otherwise the individual may find himself enmeshed in Judgement visions relating to *karma* associated with his personality, debased sexual fantasies, or other projections of neurosis.

To summarise the essential teaching of the *Bardo Thodol* : The Great Liberation is achieved by ego-loss or 'death of the ego'; this state may be achieved in the first *Bardo* of the Clear Light or by transcending the images of deities in the second *Bardo*. Below these levels the ego gains more and more strength, and seeks 'rebirth' in the world of the senses where it is able to assert itself once more as dominant. Most of us, said Leary, are doomed to return to normality after the journey. However, training for these levels of consciousness would allow greater familiarity with the most sacred realms of mind. Eventually the choice for Liberation would have to be taken.

However, on a more mundane level, Leary's excursions from normality into altered states of consciousness were heading for a political showdown at Harvard University. Media reports of the drug experiments conducted by the Center for Personality Research had enraged Professor Herbert Kelman, a fellow psychologist on the faculty, and also Professor Brendan Maher, who dismissed Leary's findings and believed psilocybin and LSD were dangerous drugs that should only be administered by physicians in a medical setting. The campus debate was highlighted in the media and in turn came to the notice of the Massachusetts State Narcotics Bureau. After several police investigations and a considerable amount of departmental wrangling, Timothy Leary and Richard Alpert were dismissed from Harvard University in May 1963, the first time in 300 years that faculty members had been asked to leave because of controversy surrounding current research.

Necessarily this led to a temporary parting of the ways for Alpert and Leary, although Metzner later collaborated with Leary in the International Foundation for Internal Freedom and the Castalia Foundation. Metzner also edited *The Psychedelic Review* for several years and went on to produce a number of notable books, including *The Ecstatic Adventure, Maps of Consciousness* and, most recently, *Opening to Inner Light*. He is now Professor of East-West Psychology at the California Institute of Integral Studies in San Francisco.

Richard Alpert, meanwhile, went off to India in 1967, initially to discover what the holy men of the East could make of LSD. A Californian named Bhagwan Dass took Alpert into the foothills of the Himalayas and subsequently Alpert showed his sacrament to Dass's guru, Neem Karoli Baba ('Maharaj-ji'). The holy man consumed Alpert's entire stock – 900 micrograms – and was apparently totally unaffected! Someone explained to Alpert that the sage operated in a mental space called *sahaj samadhi* which was not dependent on sources of stimulation from the bio-physical level, and Alpert realised he had found a higher source of spiritual authority than he had anticipated. The Maharaj-ji allowed Alpert to stay, providing him with a teacher, and the former Harvard professor now became Baba Ram Dass.

Dass now says that 'the only thing you have to offer to another human being, ever, is your own state of being'. He remains a Westerner, if only by heritage, and now spends much of his time communicating the spiritual truths of Indian Yoga to Western audiences. A transcript of his excellent lectures for the Menninger Foundation in Topeka, Kansas, was published in 1973 in a book titled *Doing Your Own Being*, and he has since published several other books including *Journey of Awakening* and *Grist for the Mill*, co-authored with Stephen Levine.

Leary, meanwhile, found that after his dismissal from Harvard he had become a scapegoat for the widespread political distrust of psychedelics. For many years he lived the unfortunate life of a jail escapee-cum-hunted man on the basis of an initial charge of possessing less than one ounce of marijuana. However in recent years his life has returned, dare one say it, to a state of comparative normality. Following the successful publication of *Flashbacks* in the United States in 1983 and his widely reported publicity encounters with former law-enforcement officer G. Gordon Liddy (who had arrested Leary in the mid-1960s), Leary now attracts attention primarily as a lecturer on the American campus circuit. Computers have now replaced his once all-consuming interest in psychedelics and the extraordinary days of drug research at Harvard seem like memories from another era.

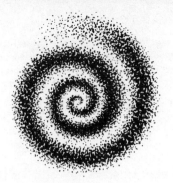

6 · Maps for Inner Space

If the early years of psychedelic research and the blossoming of hippiedom shared a certain sense of quirky eclecticism, an important finding nevertheless emerged: reliable maps of consciousness were urgently required. To their credit, Timothy Leary, Richard Alpert and Ralph Metzner surveyed the esoteric and mystical literature in some depth before selecting the *Bardo Thodol* as the basic framework for *The Psychedelic Experience*. But there were other maps relating to archetypal levels of spiritual reality as well. Metzner began to explore a range of mystical systems from both East and West and in 1970 completed a book titled *Maps of Consciousness* which compared some of the different approaches he had found most useful in charting the geography of inner space.

In this new book Metzner included outlines of the *I Ching*, Tantra, Astrology and other esoteric traditions. He agreed with Leary that the old subject–object duality was outmoded in the field of scientific observation. A scientist, particularly one dealing with intangibles like thought processes and altered states of consciousness, had to be prepared to enter his own experiments and to be his own testing ground. As a researcher himself he had long realised he would have to disregard existing behavioural models in psychology in favour of self-development systems outlined in various forms of mysticism:

The esoteric psychological schools as well as some of the oriental ones, have maintained the knowledge of the Higher, Immortal Self, the Krishna-consciousness, or Christ-consciousness, which is the teacher–knower within who can guide the person's evolutionary growth towards individuality. Concepts of what is 'normal', or 'right' or 'should be' are all image-obstructions to our receptive perception of what actually is; which can only be learned by listening-looking-sensing within. . .[1]

In the *I Ching* Metzner found an 'interesting matrix of change, that fuses the positive and negative energies' in the interplay between *yang* and *yin*. Usually the *I Ching* was used as a divinatory oracle: forty-nine yarrow stalks were taken and the heap divided in a certain way to produce alignments on a 'hexagram' pattern which could be interpreted according to a body of traditional meanings. The *I Ching* seemed to operate upon laws of balance, and since man himself was the microcosm, there was a correspondence between internal tuition (used in divinatory interpretation) and external events in the world (the macrocosm). Man could therefore use the oracle to determine appropriate courses of action at a given time.

Metzner was interested in Astrology for much the same reasons. In particular, what he termed 'the linkage between planetary and other cosmic cycles on the one hand and processes on earth, particularly in man, on the other' concerned him most. It was thus not planetary influences *per se* which should be considered but the symbolism of their movements in the heavens describing cycles and 'geophysical rhythms' affecting man in the form of accident proneness, incidence of disease, human fertility and so on. In addition, relevant insights could be acquired into the individual personality facets which allowed the self-inquiring experimenter to recognise character traits he could 'work with or through'. It was appropriate that he should view them in this way, rather than 'obstacles in the form of *faults* given at birth'.

In exploring Tantra, the yoga of sexual eneigy, Metzner pursued further a direction begun with Leary and Alpert in their psychedelic adaptation of the *Bardo Thodol*. Particular emphasis has been laid in this branch of yoga upon *yantras* (geometrical diagrams used for visualisation processes), *mantras* (specially conceived rhythmic utterances designed to modify consciousness in a certain way) and *mudras* (special postures and gestures, especially of the upper limbs, which enable 'transformations of bodily experience through the channelling of energies' to occur). Tantra seeks to unite in man his opposite polarities – the male and female characteristics which Jung had also alluded to in the form of his animus/anima theory (the idea that women and men have complementary sexual forces active within the unconscious). The supreme state of bliss is a unity above opposites, and means of raising the Kundalini to this level had intrigued Metzner since his original study of *Bardo* states of consciousness. The Kundalini, as a union of opposites in itself, constituted the symbolic, mystical axis of man. Upon it lay certain *chakras*, or energy centres: 'the points in which psychic forces and bodily functions merge into each other or penetrate each other'. Two encapsulating lines of force, or *nadis*, were said to operate around the central nervous system or axis (*sushumna*): *ida*, the negatively charged lunar current, and *pingala*, the positive and masculine current. The special value of this mystical system in Metzner's view was that 'part of the esoteric practice of the Tantric psychologist undoubtedly consisted of increasing one's awareness of the psycho-physical field by amplifying energy flow through the *nadis*'. Another poi. t of importance was that some experimenters with psychedelics seemed to be arousing Kundalini energy without fortifying the body by Hatha Yoga techniques in the customary way employed by Tantrics.

Two other esoteric traditions also experienced a dramatic resurgency in the late 1960s as part of the mystical revival in the counter-culture, and these were the ancient Jewish Kabbalah and the medieval Tarot. In the literature of modern occultism they have tended to become entwined into a single, but complex, system. However, as with the *Bardo Thodol*, the combination of the Kabbalistic Tree of Life, with its ten stages of consciousness between Godhead and man, and the Tarot, with its symbolic pathways linking these archetypal levels, offered a comparable map of Western mystical consciousness.

THE KABBALAH AND THE TAROT

In the Kabbalistic tradition the whole of the manifested universe is said to have originated in *Ain Soph*, the hidden and infinite God-Energy which is without qualities or attributes. The Kabbalists believed that as soon as one tried to ascribe qualities to the *Ain Soph*, the sense of infinity and limitlessness would be lost.

The Tree of Life symbol, which is central to the Kabbalah, in effect describes a type of crystallisation process whereby the *Infinite* gradually becomes *Finite*. And the latter is the manifested world as we see it all around us. For the Kabbalist, though, there are intermediary stages of being, or consciousness. The *Ain Soph* thus

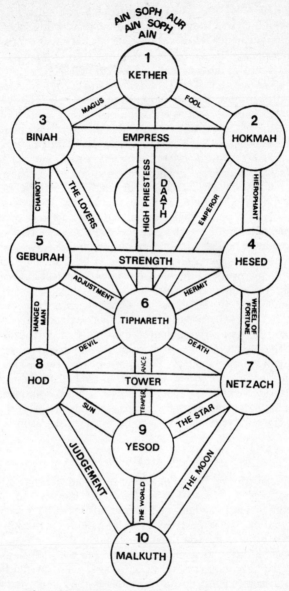

The Kabbalistic Tree of Life showing Tarot paths

Medieval Tarot cards: clockwise from top left – *The Chariot, The Star, Judgement* and *The Hermit*

reveals aspects of divinity to man, and on the Tree of Life these are represented symbolically by ten major stages called *sephiroth*, or 'spheres'. If we take these *sephiroth* to be levels of consciousness, comparable to those described in Yoga, the mystic begins his mystical ascent at the bottom of the tree and endeavours to retrace the sacred steps back to Godhead.

The ten levels are designated as follows:

Kether	The Crown, or peak of Creation
Hokmah	Wisdom (The Father)
Binah	Understanding (The Mother)
Hesed	Mercy
Geburah	Strength
Tiphareth	Harmony (The Son)
Hod	Splendour
Yesod	The Foundation
Malkuth	The Kingdom, or Earth (The Daughter)

One distinction which becomes immediately obvious is that some of the *sephiroth* have 'personal' attributes – the Father, Mother, Son and Daughter – while others are abstract (for example, Mercy). However the mystic working with this tradition regards the symbolism of each of the *sephiroth* as a type of symbolic energy process deep in the spiritual areas of the mind. The sacred images of Godhead are inherent in his being, and the various Kabbalistic meditations are aids for encountering them.

Contemporary occultists have employed the Kabbalistic Tree of Life as a framework on which to pin the archetypal symbols of all Western (and Eastern) religions. They have thus expanded its use beyond its original Judaic confines – an approach not appreciated, it has to be said, by Kabbalistic purists. In comparatively recent times, specifically since the lifetime of the French occultist Eliphas Levi (1810–75), a connection has also been made between the so-called Major Arcana of the Tarot and the ten levels of consciousness on the Tree of Life. The *sephiroth* are then regarded as levels of conscious-ness, and the Tarot cards as symbolic 'doorways' or 'paths' which lead to them.

The links between the *sephiroth* and the Tarot cards are as follows:

The World	(Malkuth-Yesod)
Judgement	(Malkuth-Hod)
The Moon	(Malkuth-Netzach)
The Sun	(Yesod-Hod)
The Star	(Yesod-Netzach)
The Tower	(Hod-Netzach)
The Devil	(Hod-Tiphareth)
Death	(Netzach-Tiphareth)
Temperance	(Yesod-Tiphareth)
The Hermit	(Tiphareth-Hesed)
Justice	(Tiphareth-Geburah)
The Hanged Man	(Hod-Geburah)
The Wheel of Fortune	(Netzach-Hesed)
Strength	(Geburah-Hesed)
The Chariot	(Geburah-Binah)
The Lovers	(Tiphareth-Binah)
The Hierophant	(Hesed-Hokmah)
The Emperor	(Tiphareth-Hokmah)
The Empress	(Binah-Hokmah)
The High Priestess	(Tiphareth-Kether)
The Magician	(Binah-Kether)
The Fool	(Hokmah-Kether)

While in the popular mind Tarot cards have been identified with the Gypsy fortune-telling tradition and are recognised as a precursor of the modern playing pack, the twenty-two Major Arcana listed above represent the archetypal cards in the pack. The other fifty-six cards, which divide into four suits – wands, cups, swords and discs – are not used meditatively. For the occultist utilising the Major Arcana in combination with the Tree of Life, either as a system of visualisations or as the basis of ritual, a real sense of spiritual growth and transcendence emerges on the journey towards the highest reaches of the Tree.

As with the Tantric polarities of Kundalini — incorporating *ida*, *pingala* and *sushumna* — the Kabbalistic framework reflects a similar balance of energies, with the Tree dividing vertically into three columns headed by the Mother archetype of Binah, the Father archetype of Hokmah and the neutral, transcendent sphere of Kether, the Crown. To this extent the Tree of Life with its ten *sephiroth* provides a remarkable counterpart in the West to the Eastern system of *chakras*, and it is worth noting that in the Kabbalah the Body of God is, in essence, also the body of man, as expressed in the dictum 'As above, so below.'

As in the East, the aim of Kabbalists and occultists following this esoteric path is first of all to overcome the constrictions of the limited, more material side of the personality and to open the mind progressively to archetypal levels of consciousness. This happens by degrees, as the mystic retraces his path back up the Tree of Life.

The correlation between the Tarot and Eastern systems of mysticism has been elegantly described by the famous scholar of religion, Heinrich Zimmer, in his book *The King and the Corpse*:

> It is my belief that the pictorial script of these [Tarot] face cards represented the degrees of an esoteric order of initiation, employing largely Christian signs, but masking the formulae of the heretical Gnostic teaching that was so widespread in Southern France up to the fifteenth century. The initiate, passing through twenty degrees of gradually amplifying enlightenment and beset by as many characteristic temptations, at last arrived at the stage of a mystical union with the Holy Trinity and this is what was symbolised in the culminating image of the series, 'The Dancing Hermaphrodite'. The Soul was the bride of the Lord, the figure of the Hermaphrodite; the two were one. The figure is immediately suggestive of the Dancing Shiva; Shiva unites in himself the Female and the Male. Such a bisexual symbol represents the embodiment in a single form all the pairs of opposites, a transcendence of the contraries of phenomenonality; and this incarnate form of forms is then conceived of as the one whose dance is the created world.[2]

Indeed, as a mythic system, the Major Arcana of the Tarot also includes all the major themes highlighted by Jung in his archetypal psychology: a personification of the descent into the underworld (the unconscious) in *The World*; the encounter with the shadow (*Death, The Beast*); archetypal representations of the Mother and Father (*The Empress* and *Emperor*); symbolic portrayals of individuation (*Temperance* and the mandala-like *Wheel of Fortune*) and the blending of sexual polarities (*The Lovers, The World, The Fool*).[3] Little surprise, then, in the fact that as a pictorial mythology, the Tarot cards would become so popular among the emerging counter-culture of the late 1960s and early 1970s.

THE RESEARCH OF JOHN LILLY AND STANISLAV GROF

During the 1970s two other figures would increasingly come to the fore in the Human Potential Movement – Dr John Lilly and Dr Stanislav Grof. Both were deeply interested in altered states of consciousness and both had evaluated the psychedelic experience as a means of providing important insights into the further recesses of the mind. Both, in turn, would have an impact on the holistic health development a decade later – Lilly as the inventor of the float-tank used for sensory isolation and meditation, and Grof as a pioneer of Holotropic Breath Therapy, a variant on Rebirthing.

Lilly had graduated from the California Institute of Technology and had received his doctorate in Medicine from the University of Pennsylvania in 1942. He then worked extensively in various research fields of science including biophysics, neurophysiology, electronics and neuro-anatomy and became well known for his research on dolphin–human relationships. This led to the publication of two books, *Man and Dolphin* and *The Mind of the Dolphin*, before his acute awareness of the sensitivity and intelligence of dolphins caused him to have ethical objections to further clinical research on these creatures. He adopted the position that it is preferable for a scientist to be his own guinea-pig before inflicting himself on his subjects.

Lilly thus began to switch his emphasis to the study of human consciousness, using his own experiences as a focal point. A few years after gaining his doctorate from the University of Pennsylvania he decided to test the idea that a person remains awake because he is bombarded with sensory stimuli. It was while working for the National Institute of Mental Health in Bethesda, Maryland, that he developed the first prototype of the float-tank. His idea was to produce an environment of solitude, isolation and confinement where sensory input was minimised as far as was humanly possible, and see what happened. Wearing a special latex rubber mask fitted with a breathing apparatus, Lilly floated naked in quiet solitude and darkness, in sea-water heated to a constant 93ºF, the temperature at which one is neither hot nor cold. In the darkness Lilly felt as if he were floating in a gravity-free dimension. He discovered that the brain compensates for the reduction of sensory stimulation by producing a marked degree of heightened *inner* awareness. 'I went through dream-like states, trance-like states, mystical states', he wrote later. 'In all of those states I was totally intact.' He remained simultaneously aware of his floating body and the nature of the experiment.[4]

This inquiry into sensory deprivation was Lilly's first scientific contact with mystical reality. It seemed to him that under these conditions the brain, or 'bio-computer', released a particular 'programme' of sensory experiences. The programme would be directly related to one's concepts and beliefs, that is to say, one would only perceive

Dr Stanislav Grof (Credit: Michael Ney)

things within the grasp of the imagination. A person with narrow conceptual confines would find himself in a barren, constricting 'space' when his mind-contents were revealed to him.

Lilly found that, potentially, sensory deprivation states offered tremendous freedom. External reality had been shut out. He could programme a mental journey to any place which his imagination could conceive – his choice of programme could take him to various specific 'spaces', or to states of consciousness representing various levels of transcendence.

During the early 1960s Lilly also took LSD for the first time, and he found that he was capable of entering mystical dimensions by this means. He had been raised as a devout Roman Catholic in his youth and he knew full well that, at death, the pure soul winged its way to God. Now, years later, while listening to Beethoven's *Ninth Symphony* under hallucinatory influence, Lilly found himself experiencing a similar 'flight of the soul'. He saw angelic beings and an aged patriarchal God seated on His Throne. The programmed learning from his youth had been re-activated by the LSD! 'Later', wrote Lilly, 'I was to realise that the limits of one's belief set the limits of the experience.'

Sometimes on his inner journeys Lilly contacted entities he called his 'two guides'. However, he resists describing these beings beyond indicating that they represented a particular type of direction and knowledge applicable only to his own wanderings on the astral planes. On occasions they appeared to epitomise his higher self talking down to the more constricted personality, showing the way towards more integrated being. At other times they took the form of 'karmic' conscience, reminding Lilly that he had commitments to his friends and family, and could not be an inner-planes drop-out without dire consequences.

As he continued to explore the various states of inner space, Lilly also began to seek what he called a 'safe place', a point of reference. Lilly's was the dark and silent void of the water tank – 'absolute zero point' – a place 'out of the body, out of the universe as we know it.' Before him were endless planes of possibilities barred only by the limits of the imagination.

On one occasion Lilly found himself in a space which he called the 'cosmic computer'. It seemed to him that he was a very small and insignificant part of *someone else's* macro-computer, in rather the same way that Jorge Luis Borges writes of an individual 'dreamed' into reality by the power of another person's imagination. Lilly sensed tremendous waves of energy, of the same intensity as those described as pertaining to the *Bardo* of the Secondary Clear Light. However, there was no sense of well-being or order. He found himself in total terror, in a whirlpool of swirling, meaningless energy, a loveless cosmic dance with 'no human value'.

Afterwards Lilly thought over his conceptions of the origin of the physical universe, which had been formulated during his scientific training. There had been no room here for mystical trance elements, or doctrines of 'love' and 'meaning'. His negative *Bardo* vision showed that a new programme was necessary. He had failed to acknowledge the energies of the Godhead working through him.

Subsequently Lilly had discussions with Alan Watts about Eastern mysticism. At Esalen he talked over the merits of Gestalt Therapy with Fritz Perls and Ida Rolf and here too he met Baba Ram Dass, who had returned from India.

Dass introduced him to various yogic techniques and the *sutras* of Patanjali. A major consequence of this was that Lilly perceived that if he wished to find Union with the Infinity of the Void he would have to stand back from both the programmer and the programme. He would have to see his results and frameworks in a new light, for the twofold division of seer and seen could no longer apply in a state of absolute Unity. He would later write, 'Beyond transcendence is an infinite variety of unknowns. . . . Beyond these unknowns, now unknown, is *full complete Truth.*'

For Lilly, this meant that even when we hold to a set of beliefs, they must always remain open-ended, for they cannot hope to encompass the transcendent unknown and contain it within finite expressions and concepts.

With Oscar Ichazo, the Chilean mystic who headed the 'mystery school' known as Arica, Lilly also discussed negative spaces. It would be most appropriate for the person seeking full mystical consciousness to have an automatic means of escaping the negative faculties of the inner planes of mind. Ralph Metzner had learned a technique of 'fire yoga' for burning out these obstacles to Unity, and Lilly called the process he learned 'the burning of Karma'. A high degree of concentration was called for – the negative qualities were seized upon and ruthlessly exhumed in transcendentally negative spaces, where they would never again exert any influence. No longer would they register on the map of inner consciousness.

Ichazo's system was based substantially on the teachings of Gurdjieff, and focused on degrees of spiritual awakening in man. In an interview in *Psychology Today* Ichazo claimed that one of his major aims was to destroy ego-dominated thoughts. When the ego or a society of egos reap the full hell they have sown in their quest for false security and status, they come to the point of collapse and rebirth. The collapse comes at the moment when the ego games are completely exposed and understood: illusion is shattered, subjectivity is destroyed, karma is burned. For Ichazo the decline of society brings with it the first moment of enlightenment.

Its roles and programmes are suspended. The only thing left is the *first Satori*.

Lilly had come to Ichazo for an alternative to current scientific conceptual frameworks, at a time when mounting drug hysteria in the United States made worthwhile research into LSD impossible. It was Ichazo who provided Lilly with a structure of the positive and negative states of consciousness from *Satori* through to *anti-Satori*. Like archetypal images, these vibrational levels were 'definitely part of our human heritage', and 'available to most of us'.

In Table 1 overleaf I have summarised the main divisions of consciousness according to Gurdjieff/Ichazo/Lilly. Beside them are the corresponding levels of consciousness according to both Kundalini/Tantric Yoga and the Kabbalah. They are fruitful grounds for comparison.

As with Dr John Lilly, Dr Stanislav Grof similarly became involved in the Human Potential Movement following years of research into psychedelics and unusual states of consciousness.

Born in Prague in 1931, Grof studied medicine and in due course received his PhD from the Czechoslovakian Academy of Science. In 1954 he began research into the psychotherapeutic uses of LSD – a controversial line of enquiry which he continued after migrating to the United States in 1967. Dr Grof worked in Baltimore at the Maryland Psychiatric Research Center and then became an assistant professor at John Hopkins University. One of his particular fields of interest was research into the use of psychedelics for easing the pain of terminal cancer patients. However he also conducted studies with depressed and alcoholic patients, schizophrenics, narcotic drug addicts and people suffering from psychosomatic illnesses.

However, Grof soon discovered that his research was leading him into deeper levels of consciousness than he expected. Reflecting on this during an interview in 1984 he said:

I was brought up and educated as a Freudian analyst and so when we started doing the LSD work I expected that we would mostly be working with biographical material. I was looking for a tool that would somehow bring out the unconscious material much faster, so that it would deepen and intensify psychoanalysis. To my surprise people would not stay in the biographical domain which, according to Western psychology, is considered to be the only domain available – memories from child-hood and the individual unconscious. Without any programming, and actually against my will, my subjects started moving into realms that hadn't been chartered in psychoanalysis at all. The first encounter was powerful. . . death and birth. People started having sequences of dying

83

TABLE 1

Lilly/Gurdjieff level of consciousness	Description	Yoga	Kabbalah
+ 3 Classical Satori	Death of the ego Consciousness transforms itself to a Universal level Union with the Godhead	*Sahasrara* (*Chakra:* above head)	Kether
+ 6 Buddha Consciousness	Ego-consciousness reduced to a very small point Direct communication at the level of Essence Astral projection/ encounters with spiritual beings	*Ajna* (*Chakra:* head)	
		Visuddha (*Chakra:* neck)	Daath
+ 12 Christ Consciousness	Cosmic love and Divine grace Joy in the company of others Perception of the aura	*Anahata* (*Chakra:* centre of chest)	Tiphareth
+ 24 'the basic professional state'	Control of the bio-computer Ability to act knowledgeably and freely within certain 'programmes'	*Manipura* (*Chakra:* lower belly)	
		Svadhisthana (*Chakra:* lumbar region) *Muladhara* (*Chakra:* genitals)	Yesod
+ 48 Normal Consciousness	Rational behaviour openness and 'neutrality' receptivity in human interaction	(*Chakra:* feet)	Malkuth

84

and feeling reborn, frequently with details from their biological birth. But this experience of death then reversed and became like a gateway into the transcendental, the archetypal – the transpersonal as we call it now. All this material emerged as a great surprise for me.[5]

As a result of these findings in his LSD research, Grof began to develop a model of the human mind which could accommodate these new elements. He now came to the view that there were basically four levels in the psychedelic encounter with the mind. The first of these, experienced at the most superficial level, involved sensory phenomena – an intensification of colours and geometrical patterns and often increased awareness of sounds, humming, chimes and so on. The next level was what Grof calls 'biographical', and its content included unresolved conflicts from one's present life, childhood problems and occasionally traumatic memories from an earlier period in one's life – diphtheria, whooping cough, cases of near drowning, major operations or injuries, and so on. These, said Grof, were the unfinished gestalts or unresolved conflicts which needed to be brought to the surface and worked through. Proceeding still deeper, however, one now came to the third level, that of perinatal experiences. These related to different phases of the birth experience and, as Grof wrote in *Realms of the Human Unconscious*, were a manifestation of a deep level of the unconscious that is clearly beyond the reach of classical Freudian techniques.

In particular Grof believed he had located certain 'matrices', or experiential patterns, relating to the processes of birth and the intra-uterine existence. Grof comments on this in his book *The Human Encounter with Death*, co-authored with Dr Joan Halifax:

LSD subjects frequently refer to the sequences of agony, death and birth (or rebirth) that are so characteristic for this area as a reliving of their actual biological birth traumas. Others do not make this explicit link and conceptualise their encounter with death and the death–rebirth experience in purely philosophical and spiritual terms. Even in this latter group perinatal experiences are quite regularly accompanied by a complex of physical symptoms that can best be interpreted as related to biological birth. It involves a variety of physical pains in different parts of the body, feelings of pressure, suffocation, drastic changes in skin colour, tremours, seizure-like muscular charges, cardiac distress and irregularities, profuse sweating, hypersecretion of mucus and saliva, and nausea. LSD subjects also assume postures and move in sequences that bear a striking similarity to those of a child during various stages of delivery. In addition, they frequently report images of, or identification with, foetuses and newborn children. Equally common are various neonatal feelings and behaviour, as well as visions of female genitals and breasts.[6]

In particular, Grof recognised four important processes of perception at the perinatal level of consciousness. The first of these was associated with the intra-uterine bond of the foetus to the mother, a type of 'symbiotic unity' Grof believed was reflected in LSD experiences as feelings of cosmic unity, tranquillity, bliss, and transcendence of time and space.

The second level was related to the first clinical stage of biological delivery, a process characterised by muscular uterine contractions while the cervix is closed. Grof believes the LSD correlate at this level is what he calls the 'experience of cosmic engulfment, or the sensation of 'no exit', an often terrifying time for the patient who feels overwhelmed by increasing levels of anxiety, unseen sources of danger and sometimes a strong sense of lurking evil. On occasion the LSD subject senses that he or she is about to be swallowed by a frightening monster or threatened by other dangerous creatures. There is often a feeling of being trapped, or caged in a torturous domain, an obvious correlation with Hell states.

The third level is associated in the birth process with the second stage of delivery, when the cervix is dilated. Here, although the uterine contractions are still continuing, the open cervix offers the prospects of survival, albeit through a process of struggling along the birth canal. Grof associates this, in the LSD experience, with death–rebirth struggles, and notes that at this time the subject can still experience a frightening encounter with repulsive materials – eating faeces, drinking blood and urine, and so on. However, there is an accompanying feeling of a long-term goal, the distinct impression that transcendence is possible. Grof links this phase, in religious terms, with Purgatory.

The fourth level, or experiential pattern, is the experience of death and rebirth, linked in the birth process with the actual birth of the child. After the birth struggle is over and the child is born, there is a profound sense of relief and relaxation. LSD subjects entering this phase, meanwhile, report 'visions of blinding white or golden light and a sense of liberating decompression and expansion. The universe is perceived as indescribably beautiful and radiant; individuals feel cleansed and purged, and talk about redemption, salvation, or union with God.'[7]

While one could take the position that these correlations between the birth process and the patterns of consciousness accessed through LSD are coincidental, Grof does not believe this to be the case:

> There are indications that the reliving of birth in LSD sessions might be associated with chemical changes in the body that represent a replica of the situation at the time of delivery, as exemplified by low oxygen saturation of blood, biochemical indicators of stress, and specifics of the carbohydrate metabolism. Even more astounding is the fact that on occasion LSD subjects reliving their birth report experiences reflecting the sensations, emotions and sometimes even the thoughts of their mothers at the time of their delivery. Many individuals volunteered independently their insights that the child and mother represent at this time a symbiotic unity not only biologically, but also experientially. All these observations, as implausible as they might appear from the point of view of the present medical beliefs about neurophysiological and mental functioning of the foetus, are sufficiently consistent and convincing to be considered clinical reality.[8]

Perhaps even more important than this, however, is Grof's belief that the perinatal experiences in turn can lead towards an even more profound level of the mind – that vast domain we have called the 'transpersonal'.

As mentioned earlier, 'transpersonal' means transcending the personal, that which is beyond the usual body/ego framework. It also refers to experiences going back to the womb, ancestral memories, Jungian archetypes, mythological sequences and past-life recall: experiences which transcend spatial boundaries rather than temporal boundaries.

It is in this area that Grof finds a link between mystical states and the principles of quantum physics – both of which emphasise the interconnectedness of all forms in the manifested universe. The sense of separation, of distinctiveness, says Grof, simply falls away at this level of awareness:

> Here the mandatory boundaries of the body seem to be melting and the person has the experience, perhaps, of fusing with other people, or becoming other people, becoming animals, becoming plant life and, in some cases, having telepathic experiences. Sometimes, too, there are mythological or archetypal sequences, portraying something that this culture would not normally regard as part of objective reality or the phenomenal world.[9]

Grof discusses these aspects in more detail in his important article 'Modern Consciousness Research and the Quest for a New Paradigm':

> There exists a group of paranormal phenomena that can be described in the same terms – as extensions of consciousness within the framework of 'objective reality'. In the case of precognition, clairvoyance and clairaudience, astral projection, 'time travel' and telepathy, it again is not the content of these experiences that is extraordinary, but the way of acquiring certain information or perceiving a certain situation that according to common sense and the existing scientific paradigms should be beyond our reach.
>
> The theoretical challenge represented by these observations is further augmented by the fact that transpersonal experiences that reflect various aspects of the phenomenal world as we know it occur in psychedelic states on the same continuum and often in combination with phenomena which are not part of the agreed-upon world view in the West. Many of the experiences of this kind could be subsumed under the general term of *archetypal phenomena* in the Jungian sense. LSD subjects frequently report that in their transpersonal sessions, they had a vivid and authentic sense of confrontation or identification with archetypes representing generalised biological, psychological and social types and roles; these can reflect various levels of abstraction and different degrees of generalisation. The Old Wise Man, Good Samaritan, Conqueror, Martyr, Fugitive, Outcast, Tyrant, Fool, or Hermit are examples of more specialised archetypal images. The most general archetypes always have strong elements of numinosity, as exemplified by the Great Mother, Terrible Mother, Father, Child-King, Great Hermaphrodite, Animus and Anima, or Cosmic Man. Frequently transpersonal experiences of this kind have concrete cultural characteristics and take the form of *specific deities, demons, demigods and heroes*. Sometimes instead of experiencing individual images, LSD subjects have a sense of participating in *complex mythological, legendary or fairytale sequences* from various cultural traditions. Quite common also are experiences of *encounters with spirits of deceased human beings and suprahuman spiritual entities*. The most generalised and universal experiences of this kind involve identification with the *consciousness of the Universal Mind* and with the *Supracosmic and Metacosmic Void*.[10]

After over 20 years of LSD research Dr Grof clearly believes he has uncovered valuable patterns for consciousness research, and his unique work has not gone unnoticed. Pulitzer Prize-winning scientist Carl Sagan noted in *The Dragons of Eden* that 'Grof probably has more scientific experience in the effects of psychedelic drugs on patients than anyone else', and distinguished parapsychologist Dr Stanley Krippner has referred to Grof as the 'world's foremost psychedelic researcher'. This recognition, however, could do little to make the LSD controversy disappear in the mid-1970s when the issue of psychedelic therapy was coming to a climax. As we will see in the following chapter, much of the impetus for the emergence of the holistic health perspective had to do with the need for finding non-drug methods for exploring inner states of being. If psychedelics were not politically, medically and psychologically acceptable, even in the hands of specialists, there had to be other therapeutic modalities for exploring and integrating body, mind and spirit.

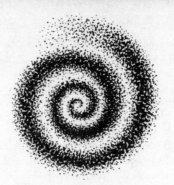

7 · THE HOLISTIC PERSPECTIVE

Dr Stanislav Grof's particular solution to the controversy with LSD was to develop an alternative therapeutic approach which did not utilise psychedelics. Grof began to shift his emphasis towards what he now calls 'Holotropic Breath Therapy', an approach which resembles the more widely known technique of 'Rebirthing'. The latter was developed by Leonard Orr in California during the early 1970s, and both Rebirthing and Holotropic Breath Therapy derive substantially from *Pranayama* – the Indian Yoga of breath – which employs a connected breathing rhythm to produce an altered state of consciousness. In both therapies the subject lies horizontally in a comfortable position with a facilitator, or helper, sitting nearby to assist in any experiential crisis. The session begins as the subject engages in rhythmic in-and-out breathing, with no pauses in between. As Orr has written: 'You merge with your breath, flowing, glowing, soaring, relaxing profoundly, your mind melting into your spirit, surging, awakening your inner being and the quiet sounds of your soul. . .'

In Holotropic Breath Therapy, however, the technique is somewhat more intense and the results more sudden and dramatic. The breathing is accompanied by recorded music which is chosen to reflect different phases of the cathartic process. As Grof explains, 'The music is the vehicle itself, so at the beginning we start with

90

some very activating, powerful music. Then, maybe an hour into the session, we move into a kind of culminating, "breakthrough" type of music – for example using the sounds of bells or similar, very powerful, transcendental sounds'.[1] His musical selections are very varied, including African tribal rhythms, Sufi chants, Indian ragas, Japanese flutes and various forms of ambient music.

Paradoxically, the type of hyperventilation breathing employed in the Holotropic approach actually reduces the amount of oxygen transmitted to the cortex of the brain, producing a natural 'high'. The technique simulates the experience of mystics who live in high altitudes where the air is more rarefied and is therefore ideal, as Grof himself says casually, for those who can't make the trip to the Himalayas! However, more importantly, Grof has found that Holotropic breathing, like LSD psychotherapy, can resolve profound emotional problems associated with the birth process, and then open out into the transpersonal dimension. The Holotropic experience, says Grof, can be similarly, 'very beneficial, very transforming and very healing. Many people tell us after a session like this that they have never been so relaxed in their whole life.'

It is characteristic that Grof's emphasis should have switched to the East, for this trend has been a marked feature of both the Human Potential Movement and the New Age in recent years.

Without doubt, during the late 1970s and on into the 1980s, the most common response of many who had come through the psychedelic era and who now wanted non-drug ways of attaining comparable states of consciousness was to turn to the East, for its rich knowledge of mysticism and spiritual states of consciousness. And, in particular, there were practical techniques of meditation one could learn and practise in order to experience these states of mind, first-hand. It also became widely apparent that meditation was extremely compatible with the concept of holistic health. Not surprisingly, the notion of addressing not only physical dimensions of disease but also mental, emotional and spiritual causes of illness and malaise became, and still remains, an increasingly popular approach for adapting to the stressful environment we live in.

MEDITATION

A widespread misconception about meditation is that it is a type of passive introversion, a peaceful but ineffectual form of self-centredness. In fact, meditation is quite different from this and as a technique of mind control has very positive benefits for health

– increasing a sense of inner calm, heightening one's powers of creativity and decision-making, and decreasing mental tension and negative emotions. Accordingly, many ailments that are stress-related can be eliminated or reduced by meditation, including migraine and tension headaches, high blood pressure, heart complaints and menstrual cramps.

Meditation became increasingly popular in the West, primarily as a result of the widespread interest in the teachings of Maharishi Mahesh Yogi and the Transcendental Meditation (TM) movement. Several million residents of the United States have since learned some form of meditation and the practice is also very popular in Britain, Germany, Australia and other Western countries. The appeal of meditation is that it broadens one's sense of being. Personal anxieties, fears and tensions, which so often underlie disease, acquire a diminished status and are less all-consuming than they might have seemed before. As Baba Ram Dass was moved to say during one of his lectures: meditation frees your awareness and opens new horizons of being.

There are basically two approaches to meditation. The first focuses on powers of concentration, the second emphasises detached awareness.

The 'concentration' approach requires that the attention be focused on a meditative symbol, a sound or chant, or a body process like breathing or the beat of the heart. Sometimes sacred mantras like *Hare Krishna* or *Om Namah Shivaya* ('I honour my inner state') are used. In some forms of concentration-meditation the teacher gives the pupil a mantra on which to meditate, twice a day. The idea is to turn the processes of thought inward until the mind transcends thought itself.

In the approach which utilises 'detached awareness' the focus is on what is happening *now*. The task is not so much to elevate consciousness to a 'higher state' but to become increasingly aware of the present moment. From this position one gains a more profound perception of the flux of life, and the ebb and flow of human experience.

The work *Visuddhimagga* – the Path to Purification – by the fifth century monk Buddhaghosa, describes the meditative approach from the Buddhist viewpoint, and in some respects it contains both approaches summarised above. One of the major disciplines of the Buddhist meditator is to eliminate distractions, with the aim of eventually attaining a 'unification of mind'. As the practitioner learns to meditate for a long period such factors as agitation, scepticism and doubt disappear and a feeling of one-pointedness (bliss) begins to dominate. The meditator beccomes absorbed in thought, a process known as *jhana*, and moves deeper and deeper, finally acquiring an awareness of the Infinite One-ness which underlies all manifestation. Many Buddhists, however, regard the pursuit of various *jhana* levels as secondary to the Path of Mindfulness which leads, finally, to *nirvana*. The meditator learns to break out of stereotypes of thought and perceives every moment of the everyday reality as if it were a new event. The ego becomes much less important and the manifested universe is seen to be in a state of total and ever-changing flux. This leads in turn to a sense of detachment from the world of experience, an abandonment of all desires and self-interest, and finally the dissolution of the ego itself.

The growth of interest in meditation in the 1970s necessarily brought with it an increasing desire among some psychologists, doctors and research scientists to understand more about the states of mental awarenesss it was enhancing. It was clear, for example, that on one level meditation could produce a deeply felt sense of relaxation which reduced physical tension and stress. An example of this was provided by Dr Syed Abdullah, a New York psychiatrist, who reported a case of a 53-year old woman whom he had treated for asthma by prescribing simple breathing techniques and meditation. Gradually she learned to control her bronchial spasms and to eliminate the complaint. However she also suffered from atopic eczema, and discovered to her delight that when she concentrated her attention on her skin condition that she was able to heal it also.[2]

More specifically, there was also renewed interest in the sorts of brain-wave patterns associated with meditative consciousness and ways of monitoring these states. This led in turn to the development of the techniques and health-applications of biofeedback.

BIOFEEDBACK

Biofeedback is literally 'feedback from the body'. It makes use of electronic instruments to monitor body functions, especially those related to muscle tension, brain-wave activity, skin temperature and electrical skin response.

Biofeedback was developed in the United States by Dr Joe Kamiya, who monitored subjects' *alpha* brainwaves (8–13 cycles per second) using an electroencephalograph (EEG) device. His machine produced a pleasant sound when the subject attained certain levels of *alpha* and encouraged the person to maintain that state. Among other things, Dr Kamiya was interested in researching the alpha-wave connection with mystical states of consciousness, meditation and inner awareness.

Since Dr Kamiya's initial experiments in 1958, there have been a number of biofeedback studies undertaken at different research establishments including the Menninger Institute in Kansas and the laboratories of Dr Maxwell Cade in England where mystics and yogis skilled in mind control have subjected themselves to scientific testing. Much of this research has had to do with 'autonomic' body functions: processes normally regarded as involuntary. It now appears that biofeedback can be used to train subjects to monitor, and exercise a degree of control over, autonomic body functions like heartbeat and blood pressure.

In India in 1979, Swami Satya Moorthi, a yogi aged 102, took part in a biofeedback experiment in which he endeavoured to stop some of his body functions and then retrigger them. Monitored by medical technicians, including Dr Y.G.Mathur, a chest specialist from Delhi, Swami Moorthi demonstrated that in a state of meditative trance he could stop his heart beating for an extended period. Over a 90-hour phase he gradually reduced his body temperature from 31°C to 26.8°C, said to be the lowest reading ever recorded for a live human being. After 192 hours, the Swami emerged from his remarkable meditation 5.5 kg lighter.

On a less esoteric level, biofeedback is now used in many hospitals to monitor and treat migraines, gastro-intestinal disorders, high blood pressure, tension states and heart disease. Patients in Baltimore City Hospital, for example, now learn how to monitor their heart conditions after being attached to a cardiotachometer which produces coloured light signals. In the same manner as driving a car, these patients learn to slow their heartbeat down when the red light comes on, and increase it when a green light shows. Several devices also exist which provide light signals which intensify as a patient relaxes. These can be used to overcome hypertension, migraine headaches and similar complaints.

Dr Maxwell Cade believed that four different states of mind had specific feedback correlations. In November 1974 he presented his findings to the Society for Psychosomatic Research at the Royal College of Physicians.

Cade had measured the electrical skin response (ESR) in a group of subjects to test for levels of tension. The more sweat monitored on the palm of the subjects' hands, the more tension present. At the same time, Cade also monitored the EEG pattern for *alpha*, *beta*, *theta*, and *delta* wave patterns in the right and left hemispheres of the brain.

By then it had been generally established that *alpha* is associated with relaxation and meditation, *beta* with active thinking, *theta* with dream-like imagery and creative thought, and *delta* with deep sleep. Cade found that the following correlations emerged:

1. Tense body/tense mind: low ESR/*beta* EEG= panic

2. Relaxed body/relaxed mind: high ESR/*alpha* and *beta* EEG= meditation

3. Aroused body/relaxed mind= mediumistic trance

4. Relaxed body/aroused mind: high ESR/*alpha, beta* and *theta* EEG= Zen meditation

The equipment used in biofeedback laboratories is now highly sophisticated and includes complex meters for sensitive monitoring of skin temperature, electrical skin resistance, muscle tension and brain-wave activity. Arguably the most advanced EEG biofeedback machine produced to date is the Mind Mirror, a device which Cade's colleague Geoffrey Blundell developed to measure the rhythms from each side of the brain and then allow the blend of the two to be seen as a visual pattern. Basically, the Mind Mirror features a screen with light-emitting diodes arranged into banks of twelve rows, monitoring left and right hemisphere activity. There are *beta, alpha, theta* and *delta* indicators which allow for a highly sensitive interpretation of the mental state of the person engaged in the biofeedback experiment.

Expressed simply, biofeedback is a technological route to self-awareness. Body functions that were previously thought to be involuntary become to some extent voluntary as subjects learn an increasing degree of self-awareness and develop self-regulatory responses.

HEALTH FOR THE WHOLE PERSON

Notwithstanding the inroads that were being made in the 1970s in correlating different brain-wave patterns with specific states of mystical and altered states of consciousness, a much broader-based outlook was also gathering momentum, and that was the Holistic Health perspective itself. The 1960s consciousness had brought in its wake an important aftermath – a widespread awareness that inner states of being were vitally important in any definition of essential human-ness. This, of course, was the crucial focus of both

Humanistic and Transpersonal psychology, but it began to influence concepts of health and medical care as well. A characteristic definition, epitomising the new orientation, appeared in a work titled *Dimensions of Humanistic Medicine*, published in San Francisco in 1975. Here the authors described human health care in a way which acknowledged the *total* human being, both as a physical and spiritual being:

> A person is more than his body. Every human being is a holistic, interdependent relationship of body, emotions, mind and spirit. The clinical process which causes the patient to consult the medical profession is best understood as this whole and dynamic relationship. The maintenance of continued health depends on harmony of this whole.[3]

The idea of tapping one's own innate healing potential, of regarding the process of overcoming disease as a learning experience, and of becoming more self-reliant, were all perceptions that had spilled over from the earlier years of Maslow, Sutich and Esalen.

Whereas, in more traditional styles of Western medical practice, patients were generally regarded as dependent on the doctor and illness was considered a complaint to be eliminated, the new focus was on helping the patient to become more knowledgeable about his condition and to participate in the healing process. The complaint could then provide the patient with insights and opportunities for self-discovery. The old concept was that health could be defined as the absence of disease and that in states of illness one should pay attention primarily to the specific symptoms, or body parts, which had 'gone wrong'. Now, however, the emphasis was being placed on health as a positive and natural state of human wellbeing, with the whole person, and not just the symptom or organ as the subject of the medical enquiry. There was also an increasing recognition that the frame of reference should not just be purely physical, but should also encompass mental and emotional aspects of health and even such areas as spiritual values, the search for personal meaning, and the integrative nature of religious beliefs. And there was a shift away from *curative* medicine towards the *prevention* of illness. This brought with it the long overdue acknowledgement that such self-help factors as sensible nutrition, regular exercise and personal preventive health-care measures were all vital considerations in avoiding illness. It was a matter, as Schutz and Perls had stressed at Esalen, of taking substantial responsibility for your own health care. And where treatments *were* required from a doctor, they would preferably be intended not just to repress isolated symptoms, but to help restore balance and integration to the organism as a whole.

Most importantly, there was a dramatic switch away from synthetic medicines towards natural remedies, whenever they were available. The emphasis in the Holistic Health Movement was now on the remarkable capacity of the human organism to rectify imbalance and engage in a self-healing process. 'Natural' modalities, like naturopathy, acupuncture, shiatsu and homeopathy, which stimulated healing processes from within the organism itself, were to be preferred whenever possible. This brought with it a new sensibility that healing should be as non-intrusive as possible, that synthetic chemicals and other 'unnatural' agents were to be totally avoided, or used only as a last resort.

However, potentially the most far-reaching suggestion of the Holistic Health proponents was that mind, body and spirit were necessarily interrelated and that health-care should henceforth have to acknowledge all of these dimensions in the future. It was a proposal which hinted more than a little at mysticism, and which still attracts widespread resistance among many doctors. Indeed, the whole issue of the interrelatedness of mind and body has only recently begun to gain consideration in orthodox medical circles. Until quite recent times, any specific links between mind (*pysche*) and body (*soma*) in relation to the cause of disease have been difficult to demonstrate clinically, even though many individual doctors have believed for some time that such connections exist.

The late Professor Hans Selye of the University of Montreal, an important figure in the Holistic Health Movement, regarded stress as an extremely important factor underlying illness. However, he was keen to point out that stress should not necessarily be equated with *intensity* of lifestyle. Stress, he believed, was best thought of as deriving from the perception of events in our lives, and was therefore a reflection of our ability to deal with the demands of those events. Stress could be measured by such factors as general irritability, depression, high blood pressure, impulsive and aggressive behaviour, inability to concentrate, accident proneness, emotional tension, sexual problems, insomnia, migraine headaches and a variety of other symptoms. Selye noted, too, that people react differently to the demands made upon them. We all learn to adapt to pressures, but stress arises when the process of coping begins to fail. We then have to develop daily priorities for regaining equilibrium – by slowing down or altering the pace of life, and so on. Otherwise we risk a breakdown of health beginning, perhaps, with relatively minor conditions like skin complaints and intestinal upsets but leading possibly to more serious illnesses.

Studies have been made to determine whether stress is related to the incidence of cancer and heart attacks, and consideration has been given to the question: are certain personality types more susceptible?

As early as 1959 the Californian cardiologists Dr Ray Rosenman and Dr Meyer Friedman put forward the hypothesis that a behavioural pattern known as 'Type A' correlated with the likelihood of heart disease. Such a person was extremely competitive and aggressive, scheduled more and more activities into less and less time, was in too much of a hurry to derive any sense of beauty from the environment, did not delegate tasks easily, exhibited explosive speech patterns, had trouble sitting and doing nothing, and was given to lip-clicking, head-nodding, fist-clenching and other related traits. The Type A person, in a business setting, might appear to be extremely productive and full of confidence, but underneath felt inferior and was prone to failure.[4]

More recently, a panel of twenty-five noted American cardiologists, epidemiologists and psychologists convened under the auspices of the National Heart, Lung and Blood Institute and concluded that the evidence for the Rosenman/Friedman hypothesis was substantial and that such a personality type *does* have a high risk of coronary heart disease.

A similar relationship seems to exist between psychological factors, stress, and the outbreak of cancer. According to Dr Charles Garfield of the Cancer Research Institute at the University of California, 'The evidence demonstrating that malignant processes are related to certain psychological conditions is formidable'.

This opinion is shared by Dr Lawrence Le Shan, former head of the psychology department at the Institute of Applied Biology, and now a leading advocate of meditation and holistic health. After studying 250 cancer patients and administering personality tests, Le Shan compared them with 150 non-cancer subjects. The following factors emerged:

- 77 per cent of cancer subjects but only 14 per cent of healthy subjects showed extreme tension over the loss of a close relative or friend.

- 64 per cent of cancer subjects as opposed to 32 per cent non-cancer subjects, showed signs of not being able to adequately express anger, resentment and aggression towards other people, but bottled up their feelings instead.

98

- 69 per cent of cancer patients had low personal esteem and culpability while only 34 per cent of the control group showed this characteristic.

Le Shan also found that, typically, cancer patients had experienced a major emotional trauma six to eighteen months prior to the development of the disease.

Dr Carl Simonton, a physician specialising in the holistic treatment of cancer, has extended the hypothesis of Doctors Friedman and Rosenman beyond heart patients, and believes that there is also a 'cancer' personality. The most pronounced characteristics are:

- A tendency to hold resentment and a marked inability to forgive.

- An inclination towards self-pity.

- A poor ability to develop and maintain meaningful, long-term relationships.

- A very poor self-image.

Dr Simonton has placed great emphasis on Professor Selye's discovery that chronic stress suppresses the immune system, since this is the mechanism for destroying or keeping at bay the cancerous cells present in the body. During the 'May Lectures' held in London in 1974, Dr Simonton stated:

All human beings have cancer cells within them.. The problem is not the cancer cells but the breakdown of the body's ability to deal with them and rid itself of disease. I see cancer, therefore, as having much in common with diseases like tuberculosis, the common cold and so forth. We are continually exposed to many dangerous agents both from within and without, but it is only when we become susceptible to them that the disease actually develops.[5]

One of the Simonton's most diistinctive techniques, as an adjunct to orthodox radiation therapy, has been the use of guided visualisation and relaxation to enable the patient to focus on the cancerous growth. Three times a day, every day, the patient visualises the disease, the treatment and the body's own immune mechanisms (white blood cells) acting positively and victoriously over the disease. Dr Simonton has found that patients with a positive attitude towards their disease have a much more favourable clinical response to treatment than those with a poor attitude.

Dr David Bresler, who works from a holistic health centre in Los Angeles, has used similar psychosomatic techniques to reduce pain. One of his patients, a cardiologist with rectal cancer, was in excruciating agony. Dr Bresler asked him to visualise the pain and finally it emerged in the form of a large, vicious dog snapping at his spine. The patient was asked to imagine himself making friends with the dog, talking to it and patting it on the head. As the patient succeeded in this he found the pain subsiding, and after a few sessions it became quite manageable.

The Australian psychiatrist Dr Ainslie Meares who, until his recent death, spent many years of his life researching 'mind and body' considerations in disease, came to a similar conclusion as Simonton, Le Shan and Bresler. Meares had lived for a time in a Zen monastery in Japan, and had a profound respect for Oriental techniques of meditation, which he was convinced could help reduce anxiety levels in patients. Like Dr Simonton, Meares believed that the immune system held the key to whether cancer would develop or not, and he similarly felt that the immune system could be influenced by mental as well as physiological processes.

According to Dr Meares, the anxious, distressed or nervous person, a person who is not coping adequately with the stresses of his life, places increased pressure on his hormonal balance and, through his nervous and endocrine systems, produces larger amounts of cortisone than usual. Unfortunately, cortisone inhibits the body's immune system and therefore renders the body more liable to disease. Like Dr Simonton, Meares believed that we are probably all manufacturing aberrant cancer cells in our bodies but normally the immune system can overcome these problems. The person who develops cancer is one whose immune system has weakened, allowing the cancer to take hold and multiply.

Dr Meares advised his cancer patients to meditate because he was convinced that the meditation would lessen anxiety and tension, and thereby reduce the cortisone level of the body. This would then restore the balance in favour of the immune system and allow the physical organism the possibility of returning to its normal state of health.

While many orthodox doctors continue to be wary of psychosomatic treatments and cannot bring themselves to believe that meditation and visualisation could really produce a clinical effect, in recent times important insights have been provided by a new science, psychoneuroimmunology (PNI), which has gone a long way towards endorsing the Holistic Health perspective.

THE HOLISTIC PERSPECTIVE

Basically, PNI researchers are now involved in the intriguing task of investigating how the brain interacts with the body's immune cells – how the brain sends signals via the nerves to enable the body to fight disease. Since these pathways can be triggered by thoughts and emotions, such research has been useful for discovering how seemingly subjective or intangible holistic therapies like visualisation and meditation are in fact working with something physiologically real.

The new finding is that the brain and immune system constitute a closed circuit and that there is a two-way interaction between the immune system and the brain which monitors the presence of intrusive bacteria, tumours and viruses in the body.

Neuropharmacologist Dr Candace Pert, who works for the National Institute of Mental Health in the United States, believes that neuro-peptides, small protein-like chemicals made in the brain, operate rather like 'biochemical units of emotion'. The neuropeptides, which include the well-known category of endorphins, are morphine-like chemicals generated in the brain, which produce marked changes in mood. However, it also appears that neuropeptides can connect with macrophages (cells which help destroy infection and disease), influencing the speed and direction of their movement. The interaction of these two classes of chemicals in the body appears to offer a scientific explanation for an effect we all acknowledge intuitively, that our moods and state of mind can affect our state of health. For example, it may be the sheer emotional power of optimism and positive thinking which helps some people recover from seemingly 'terminal' types of illness. The reason for this is that the positive attitude itself helps to keep the immune system fighting.

Another, and more specific, insight into how holistic visualisation could work is provided by French researcher Gerard Renoux of the University of Tours in France. Renoux notes that in controlling the immune system, the brain requires co-operation between the left and right hemispheres of the brain. If there is a situation of altered symmetry, the delicate regulation of the immune system may become interrupted and the person becomes more vulnerable to disease. In the case of the therapies involving visualisation to fight illness, the imagery itself is controlled substantially by the right side of the brain, and exerrrcises which stimulate this type of activity may help to 'distract' the brain from suppressing the immune system. At the same time, the sense of positiveness and optimism helps to stimulate the left hemisphere of the brain and in so doing strengthens the immune system's response against disease.

In other words, visualisation can be a really effective therapeutic tool in bridging brain hemisphere imbalance and maximising the body's potential for regaining a state of health and wellbeing.

A similar type of finding emerged recently from research at the Medical Illness Counseling Center in Chevy Chase, Maryland. There, immunologist Nick Hall and psychologists Barry Gruber and Stephen Hersh were able to demonstrate clinically that relaxation and positive mental imagery stimulated the production of lymphocytes to fight cancer tumours more effectively, thus confirming the pioneering work of Doctors Simonton, Le Shan and Meares.

Professor Ed Blalock of the University of Texas, has summed up the current direction of psychoneuroimmunology very succinctly:

> Your classical sensory systems recognise things you can see, taste, touch, smell and hear. Bacteria and viruses have none of these qualities, so how are you going to know they are there unless the immune system lets your brain in on the secret? The immune system may be the sixth sense we've been seeking all these years. . .[6]

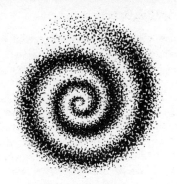

8·THE
'NEW AGE'
AND BEYOND

In recent years the popular focus has moved away from the Human Potential Movement towards its more visible but less discerning counterpart – the 'New Age'. While it is clear that the Human Potential Movement has an academic lineage which extends from present incumbents like Dr Stanislav Grof and Dr John Lilly back to Abraham Maslow, Alfred Adler, Carl Jung and William James, the New Age has been much more eclectic and undiscriminating in its pursuit of mystical consciousness. Here, with equal abandon, we find a liberal sprinkling of healing with crystals, 'chakra balancing', affirmations for prosperity consciousness and a seemingly never-ending procession of 'spiritual masters' who hold wisdom-teaching workshops or preside over well-endowed ashrams. There are executives for whom expanding consciousness really means improving the bottom line of profit-making in business and who are therefore drawn to the New Age for its promise of material abundance and an end to 'poverty consciousness'. And there are those whose sense of self-confidence is perhaps so fragile that they grasp at all manner of oracles – from divination and predictive astrology through to the fortune-telling aspects of the I Ching and Tarot (as distinct from their archetypal applications).

The New Age is also a movement with its own superstars, among them its most prominent mouthpiece, American actress Shirley MacLaine. During her New Age lecture tour in 1987, while emphasising the divine potential latent in all human beings, she would tell her audiences: 'I am God'. When a woman in New York rose from her seat to object, MacLaine is said to have replied 'If you don't see me as God, that's because you don't see yourself as God.'[1] Although such statements seem incredibly brazen at first glance, it is clear that Shirley MacLaine was intending to convey the sense that every human being is animated by the spark of Godhead. And as one writer put it, 'She believes that each person is the centre of creation and that power, wisdom and the strength to overcome resides in every individual.'[2]

This, of course, is hardly different from the message of Esalen in the 1960s – a type of humanism laced with spiritual potential. However, where the New Age seems to have crumbled in its credibility is in its bland mix of self-help, 'channelled' inspiration, confused mythologies and showbiz therapies. There is now a multi-million dollar international market in experiential workshops, lectures, crystals, relationships counselling, float tanks and rebirthing, presented in a way which has tended to trivialise the more important findings of the Human Potential Movement which preceded it. Thus we find the motivational Individual Psychology of Alfred Adler replaced on a more popular level by organisations like Est and its more recent counterpart Forum, and Dr John Lilly's original float tank prototypes adapted to promote stress-release and accelerated subliminal learning. And there are numerous workshops on loving relationships, discovering the inner child, dialoguing with the inner voice, reawakening the inner pulse, all of them variants on Carl Jung or the encounter therapies of the 1960s, albeit promoted with often extraordinary price-tags.

Nevertheless, the New Age represents a desperate spiritual yearning, an urge for inner experience, for religious frameworks which equate with the emergent holistic paradigm. Many New Agers have turned away from institutional religions because they find their doctrines too formal, their belief systems too rigid. And yet the eclecticism of the New Age can be its own worst enemy, producing an uncritical mix of ideas which flows from a real need to be 'open' to all possibilities in life – from chakras and crystals through to past incarnations in Atlantis.

'SHAMANS' OR 'MEDIUMS'?

In an attempt to make sense of the New Age for myself, I have made a distinction which delineates some of the perceptions that are now current. It seems to me that, in a broad sense, New Age devotees fall into two reasonably distinct camps. Some behave rather like shamans, and others rather like mediums – to borrow a distinction from anthropology.

In traditional native societies when shamans go on a vision-quest and enter an altered state of consciousness, they take the responsibility for their journeys and retain control of the altered state. An Eskimo or Aboriginal shaman, for example, might travel in a trance state to meet Sedna, the Sea-Goddess, or to encounter Baime, the 'All-Father', respectively, and then return with sacred information which is relevant to the tribe's future prosperity and knowledge. In the mystical state, the shaman retains full awareness and memory of what has occurred and is an intermediary between non-ordinary levels of consciousness and everyday reality.

In mediumistic cultures, on the other hand, the medium or intermediary person takes a passive role and does not retain the knowledge or memory of what has happened in the altered state – the medium is simply a channel or vessel through which information passes.

One can relate the shaman to the New Age and Human Potential Movement in this way: the person concerned is seeking new realms of experience and knowledge which extend beyond the familiar realm of 'normality'. He takes full responsibility for his experience in seeking to broaden the range of his perceptions, whatever the modality he happens to be using (rebirthing, meditation, visualisation, yoga and so on) and will endeavour subsequently to assimilate the experiences gained within his own cultural context so that, by sharing with others, he can help broaden the range of available experiential knowledge. To this extent, it seems to me, many people within the New Consciousness are behaving 'shamanically'. Some, for example, are helping develop a broader paradigm which takes in the 'new physics', archetypal psychology or global awareness. Others place particular emphasis on meditation, visualisation and other types of experience leading to spiritual fulfilment. And others are working more specifically with a range of physical or mental therapies, disciplines and practices which all contribute in some degree to enhanced self-knowledge. The core attitude, however, is that one takes the responsibility for the exploration of new perspectives and seeks, wherever possible, to be self-reliant rather than overly dependent on others.

The 'mediumistic' person withiin the New Age, however, is not seeking self-reliance but some form of authority, or 'permission', from another source. This can take many forms. There may be recourse to various types of divination – throwing the I Ching yarrow sticks, evaluating one's name and birthdate in numerology, or consulting a predictive astrologer for important decisions affecting one's personal life. Alternatively, there may be a total surrender to a dominant spiritual leader who is believed to bestow grace or a particular type of knowledge on the condition that a particular path, or sets of rules, are adhered to. The 'spirit' is then said to 'flow' into the open vessels which are the followers.

Finally, there are the 'channellers' themselves, like American New Age personality J.Z. Knight with her 35,000 year-old Atlantean warrior sage Ramtha, whose pronouncements she channels from the inner planes while in a state of trance. Among recent communications from Ramtha, channelled in November 1987 to an audience in Sydney, were that 'God is both male and female, and yet neither', that 'women only become wicked because they are afraid' and that 'if you have seen evil in another person you are the evil. If you have despised another person, you have despised their reflection because it is your own'. If Ramtha's philosophical speculations varied somewhat in their degree of profundity, there was no doubting the impact of his announcement that a giant wave would soon overwhelm coastal Sydney: several people in the audience decided then and there that they would move inland, to the relative safety of the Blue Mountains and beyond.[3]

A key distinction in the 'mediumistic' approach is that while it initially produces an undoubted openness in personal attitudes, it also reduces the sense of discrimination and healthy scepticism. It is the oracle which must be true, rather than one's own perceptions or intuitions. It is the guru or 'channelled' sage who must be heeded as an embodiment of truth because the revelations derive from a 'higher' or discarnate source. Regrettably, and all too often, the mediumistic New Age pattern results in a feeling of personal dis-empowerment – the sense that one simply cannot come to valid conclusions by drawing on one's own resources. In more sinister cases, exemplified by various extremist cults, the spiritual leader may seek to divide group against group or person against person by allocating various privileges to some followers and not to others, or by maintaining that some devotees have been 'initiated' to higher levels of insight and understanding than others. Such practices, quite clearly, are an abuse of spiritual power.

THE GURU PHENOMENON

Gurus come in all shapes and sizes, and with varying degrees of credibility. A recurring theme among gurus, both past and present, is that their teaching in some way precludes that of other, competing teachers. Perhaps the teaching is said to be 'more enlightened' or 'more ancient' than other teachings. Or the doctrine derives from a revelation which only this particular guru has earned. Invariably, there is also a distinct sense of hierarchy: there are those who know (the guru and those who have been 'initiated') and there are those who don't know (the other, newer followers). And there is usually a comparatively rigid belief system which flows from the guru's knowledge. Any competing teaching would be deemed as impure, or an adulteration.

One can recognise these symptoms in many of the religious, or quasi-religious traditions which have filtered into the New Age. And yet the guru syndrome is not confined to imported teachings from the mystical East. The phenomenon has arisen in both East and West, and has been with us for at least a century.

When Madame Helena Blavatsky founded the Theosophical Society in New York in 1875 – during an era which, like the present, was characterised by a range of spiritual belief systems like Christian Science, Spiritualism and Western Hermeticism – she claimed that the Secret Doctrine she was about to reveal represented an 'ancient wisdom'. She also maintained that she was being guided by living authorities on the inner planes, Masters who had gained perfection and were now bestowing their spiritual insights upon her. In the early years of the Theosophical Society, Madame Blavatsky claimed frequent contact with the Masters, including the alleged manifestation of mysterious letters said to have been written by them. In such a way were her spiritual 'credentials' established.

Similarly, in the late nineteenth century Hermetic Order of the Golden Dawn, which remains the principal source of many Western occult practices and was also the inspiration behind the famous Rider Tarot pack, the co-founder of the Order, MacGregor Mathers, claimed comparable channels of spiritual inspiration. Mathers called his mystical contacts 'the Secret Chiefs' and proclaimed that they had helped him from the inner planes to prepare the higher grades of ritual initiation practised in the Temple of Isis Urania. The Secret Chiefs had chosen him, he said, because of his 'profound occult archaeological knowledge' and because he was willing to pledge 'blind and unreasoning obedience' to their cause. And yet Mathers was unable to supply his followers with many specifics about these beings:

> I do not even know their earthly names. I know them only by certain secret mottoes. I have but very rarely seen them in the physical body, and on such rare occasions the rendezvous was made astrally by them at the time and place which had been astrally appointed beforehand.
>
> For my part, I believe them to be human and living upon this earth but possessing terrible superhuman powers.[4]

Similar examples of mystification abound in our own times. Sometimes the guru is elevated to a position of godliness by virtue of his claimed achievements. A recently distributed biography of Indian spiritual leader Sri Chinmoy, for example, related that:

> In 1975 Sri Chinmoy painted over 120,000 works of art depicting higher realms of meditation. His poetry and music became just as voluminous. On November 1st, 1975 Sri Chinmoy demonstrated the creative dynamism of meditation by writing 843 poems in a 24 hour period. Fifteen days later he painted 16,031 works of art in another 24 hour period. Three days later Sri Chinmoy celebrated a year in which he had completed 120,000 paintings. Since arriving in America he has composed over 5,000 songs and musical compositions, earning the praise of such notable composers as Leonard Bernstein and Zubin Mehta.[5]

Presumably, this extraordinary data about Sri Chinmoy was intended to establish him as a role model for his prospective followers. As Sri Chinmoy himself explained, 'Our goal is always to go beyond, beyond, beyond. There are no limits to our capacity because we have the infinite divine within us. Each painting, each poem, each thing that I undertake is nothing but an expression of my inner cry for more light, more truth, more delight.'[6]

However, while one could hardly fail to admire the sheer volume of his output, the effect of such statistics upon his followers would surely have been to dis-empower them, rather than to uplift them. After all, who else but Sri Chinmoy could maintain such an exalted pace of creative manifestation? The manoeuvre of out-performing all possible rivals was, by its very nature, a strategy for gaining followers to the cause. Devotees could come to his concerts to admire him, and, in particular, to gain privileged insights from his music. As a publicity notice for one of his recent concerts revealed: *'Unlike other musicians, Sri Chinmoy's music is not composed for entertainment but as a guide to higher states of awareness'*[7] [author's italics]. In other words, as the author of this statement clearly believed, Sri Chinmoy was the *only* musician capable of providing this special path to higher consciousness.

Another recent publicity advertisement in this genre described the special gifts of Elizabeth Clare Prophet who, it was announced, would speak on 'the Teachings of the Ascended Masters'. 'Empowered by the Holy Spirit', the advertisement read, 'the world's foremost woman religious leader delivers the dynamic word and wisdom of the Ascended Masters on how to heal yourself and your loved ones – body, mind and soul. Bring your problems to the altar for healing invocations. Experience the transfiguring power of the Light of God that never fails.'[8]

Prior to the demise of his ashram in Oregon, Bhagwan Shree Rajneesh also exercised a remarkable charismatic power over his followers. Each day *sannyasins* would file in procession to watch as the Bhagwan drove past in his gleaming Rolls Royce, flanked by security guards armed with Uzi semi-automatic guns. But there were also regular celebrations of Godhood at the ashram. As an advertisement in *The Rajneesh Times* for 9 August 1985 proclaimed:

Rajneeshpuram, September 4–8

A five day celebration for Mahaparinirvana Day, September 8th. Bhagwan Shree Rajneesh will speak each morning. On the evening of September 8th there will be Darshan – singing, dancing and melting into the being of the Master. Each day we will celebrate along the roadside as the Bhagwan drives by.

It would seem that double-think was clearly in evidence at Rajneeshpuram. Bhagwan's principal assistant Ma Anand Sheela, later to be jailed for conspiracy, food poisoning and attempted murder at the ashram, described during a network interview in August 1985 what Bhagwan believed he was doing, 'What he is teaching is to be individual, to become free, free of all limitations, free of all conditioning, and just become an integrated individual, a free being. . .'[9]

Bhagwan Shree Rajneesh – 'Melting into the being of the Master' (Credit: Rajneesh Foundation)

This, despite the fact that he had given each of his followers new 'spiritual names', insisted on their wearing pendants bearing his photographic image, and allowed them to wear clothing only of specific colours. Such are the paradoxes of spiritual leadership. While gurus like the Bhagwan have exhorted their followers to 'open their hearts' to their teachings, as transpersonal philosopher Ken Wilber has so wryly commented, for many New Age enthusiasts this has been at the expense of bypassing their brains.[10]

THE PROPHETS OF SELF-HELP

Quite apart from the Individual Psychology of Adler and the Human Potential Movement as a whole, the United States has also had its share of popular, 'you too can be a success' writers. Most have been self-taught and essentially self-educated. One of them was William H. Danforth, founder of the Ralston Purina Company, whose book *I Dare You!* ran through numerous editions in the 1950s. One of his chapters was 'You Can Be Bigger Than You Are', which epitomised his approach, and the book contained a potent message that everyone could help transform themselves into happier, more prosperous people.

Another work in this genre was Napoleon Hill's *Think and Grow Rich*, which announced to the reader that it would 'help you to negotiate your way through life with harmony and understanding (since) you are the master of your fate and the captain of your soul'.

110

Hill was well aware that one's fate depended on positive motivation and in turn on positive thoughts, and he believed that to implant the concept of achievement in the mind was a necessary precondition for success. To this end, argued Hill, one should 'feed his subconscious mind on thoughts of a creative nature' and visualise oneself 'on the road to success'. He advocated a type of self-hypnosis, which he called 'autosuggestion', as a way of doing this.

Hill's approach is mirrored in the New Age counterparts of 'prosperity' and 'abundance' consciousness, where devotees 'visualise' their future wealth and happiness, bolstering it all the time with 'affirmations' intended to guarantee a successful outcome. Interestingly Hill also anticipated the New Age in other ways. He maintained that to contact the Infinite Intelligence in the Universe, one's mind would have to operate with the highest 'vibrations', transcending the barriers of ordinary perception to look beyond to richer horizons.

Also in this style, but somewhat more sophisticated, was the best-selling *Psycho-Cybernetics* by Maxwell Maltz. A plastic surgeon by profession, Maltz had noticed that modifying his patients' facial features often led to positive changes in personality, so he postulated the idea that one could similarly visualise a more positive internal self-image to effect constructive change in one's life. The term 'cybernetics' itself had been coined in 1947 by mathematician Norbert Wiener and the physicist Arturo Rosenblueth and was defined as the 'science of control and communication in the animal and the machine'. Wiener and Rosenblueth were aware that biological organisms seemed to have sensors that measured deviations from set goals, which in turn provided 'feedback' that would allow such behaviour to be corrected. Basically, Maltz believed that the internal self-image one visualised could similarly help to provide a base for the personality and behaviour, and that, as long as the self-image was positively reinforced, there were potentially no limits to individual accomplishment. In this way, as one hears so often in the New Age today, people could readily learn to 'create their own reality' through a process of controlled self-transformation.

Maltz's book was undoubtedly an advance on the simpler motivational emphasis on the power of positive thinking advocated by Hill, and also by Dale Carnegie. According to Maltz, however, positive thinking by itself wasn't enough – the self-image had to be positive as well. A person endeavouring to think positively with a negative self-image could hardly hope to be successful because the two dimensions of the personality would simply fight against each other. Maltz also noted that traits like resentment and guilt were associated with a negative self-image. A person harbouring resentment, for example, was effectively allowing others to determine how he should feel or act by fixating on past events. This was completely inconsistent with striving for a positive future in which one could gain success and self-fulfilment. Guilt was also a matter of living in the past by trying to atone in the present for something 'wrong' which had occurred earlier. Maltz argued that since one could not change the past, guilt was hardly warranted. The appropriate task, emotionally, was to respond to the present situation.

Maltz believed that the main tools for changing the self-image from negative to positive were physical relaxation, imagination and hypnosis. As Maltz noted in his book:

> The proper use of the imagination can be equivalent to the beginning of a goal and a belief in this goal. And if this belief is strong enough we hypnotise ourselves with it. . . all our habits, good and bad, are daily forms of self-hypnosis. Belief is a form of creative hypnotism.[11]

The New Age counterpart of Maxwell Maltz is Shakti Gawain, bestselling author of *Creative Visualization* and *Living in the Light*. In *Creative Visualization* Gawain described a variety of exercises, meditations and affirmations to assist readers in visualising health, prosperity, loving relationships and 'the fulfilment of desires'. As she said in an interview in 1988 with New Age newspaper, *L.A.Resources*, creative visualisation was intended as 'a technique of being able to imagine having what you want in your life so that you can create the internal experience of having your life be the way you want it to be. . . . Creating that internal experience seems to open us up to creating it externally as well.'[12]

With publication of her second book, *Living in the Light*, however, Gawain moved more towards recognition of an internal guiding intelligence which could be accessed by trusting and following one's deep intuitions. During her interview she mentioned that this heightened awareness provided her with a much more qualitative approach to life: 'Moving with the energy of life and with the energy of the universe in a really spontaneous way', she said, 'is just the most exciting and wonderful way to live.'

Clearly, Gawain's approach to visualisation and intuition has taken her beyond the more specifically goals-oriented concepts of Hill and Maltz. Her vision now extends to a mix of Carl Jung's confrontation with the 'shadow' and the recognition that facing one's darker side is a vital ingredient in the planetary transformation now taking place:

> To 'live in the light' you really have to be willing to go into what you feel is the darkness. You have to face your shadow self and bring that into the light. I believe that as we are doing that individually we are also doing that on a worldwide level. The world is going through a lot of darkness, upheaval and pain, but we are becoming conscious of the things which we have repressed in the past – the things we have not been willing to deal with. Just as each of us are doing that in our own lives, it's happening on a mass consciousness level, too. I feel that if we keep having the courage, those of us who are willing to really face ourselves and really do delve into ourselves and really start living in accordance with our own inner truths to the best of our abilities, we will see that reflected in the world around us. We're just going to keep seeing that, more and more. We really live in a very exciting time.[13]

Mention should also be made here of Alexander Everett, creator of Mind Dynamics and, more recently, Inward Bound. Like Shakti Gawain, he has moved increasingly from a mental to a spiritual perspective, from an approach which initially utilised visualisation and imagination to a method which now focuses on transcending thought itself.

Everett has been an important influence on such figures as Werner Erhard (founder of est and Forum); Jim Quinn (Life Stream), Peter and Ruth Honzatko (Alpha Dynamics) and a variety of other mind control groups. And like Napoleon Hill and Maxwell Maltz before him, his initial impetus was as an exponent of 'self-improvement'.

Alexander Everett was born in Exeter, England, in 1921. At the age of 24, after returning from six years in the British Army during World War II, he managed to obtain a teaching position without any formal university training. Then, when he was 32, he established the private Shiplake School for boys, in a manor house in Henley-on-Thames, near London.

However, it is not for these achievements that he is best known in the Human Potential Movement. In 1968, having moved from England to the United States, Everett founded a system of personal development training called Mind Dynamics. Based initially in Texas and later in the San Francisco Bay Area, Everett promoted his ideas to a large audience through seminars and training programmes, explaining how the mind affected the emotions and emotions affected the body. However, despite their financial success, Everett did not find his Mind Dynamics seminars very fulfilling. What he discovered was that only around 10 per cent of people attending got a lot from what he was teaching, and they were already successful in their lives. He became increasingly concerned to develop new ways of helping a much larger percentage of the population and this led him to disband Mind Dynamics in 1973. He then undertook a spiritual search of his own.

> I travelled to India and began to realise that there was a power beyond the mind – and that was the *self*. In the West we may be inclined to call it the 'spirit' or the 'soul' – according to the religious tradition we belong – but I found out that the level of the self is perffect: there is no duality at that point. It seemed to me that if I got into that, the highest power could control the lower powers.
>
> Most people try to find out who they are through the mind and you can't do it. The mind is designed to work at the outer levels. Until you get to the inner levels there is no way you can know about these higher powers. This is the big mistake the western world makes. The mind is a lower level of consciousness. It cannot perceive that which is above.

The fruits of Everett's spiritual search were incorporated into a programme called Inward Bound which Everett now organises from his centre near Eugene, Oregon. Focusing on the idea that the God principle is within each of us, Everett now addresses four levels of human functioning – physical, emotional, mental and spiritual:

> I teach that we should *stop* thinking – that we should still the mind – and when that happens we are awakened to a Higher Source, the Eternal, the I Am, or whatever you care to call it. I train people through a process called 'centering' to make contact to be open, to wake up to this Higher Source. The idea of Inner Bound is to go to this inner state. When you do that you *know*. At the lower levels you only *think* you know.
>
> To me, God is not somebody 'out there'. God is a principle. God is within you. As you awaken to that fact, you change. In my seminars I aim for this process of centering on the God part within. . .[14]

During an interview I held with Everett in November 1988 I asked him what he felt the implications were of his approach, both within the Human Potential Movement and in a broader, international context. His response was encouraging and optimistic:

> Human potential in the ultimate sense is developing the highest state of consciousness. When you function at the lower level you want power; you want money, you want possessions, but you are on your own at

this level. However, when you open yourself to the highest level, you get a sense of One-ness, you are one with everybody else, and then you realise you can serve other people – you're not in it just for yourself.

I believe this is the big quantum leap that is coming to the planet in the next few years. Man is going to have to switch over from the lower self to the level of co-operation and service. At the moment only a minority group is doing this – but it's growing. At the moment man is Homo Sapiens – the 'wise intellectual'. Later man will be known as Homo Noeticus – the *knowing* man, who is guided by intuition and inspiration. Selfishness is out of date: co-operation is coming. People are going to have to share and work together.[15]

NEW MAPS AND MYTHOLOGIES

While the New Age has always embraced the spiritual aspects of personal growth on a reasonably popular, motivational level, the Human Potential Movement has continued to exploree these themes in a more sophisticated way. In particular, during the 1980s we have seen two exciting developments emerge: the 'Spectrum of Consciousness' model proposed by Ken Wilber and the idea that different mythologies represent a type of sacred psychology through which each of us can learn to contact the divine essence of our being.

For a man still in his early forties, Ken Wilber has earned extravagant praise for his work. Psychologist Daniel Goleman was moved to write in *The New York Times* that Wilber has joined 'the ranks of the grand theorists of human consciousness like Ernst Cassirer, Mircea Eliade and Gregory Bateson' and Dr Roger Walsh of the University of California Medical School at Irvine has called him 'the foremost writer on consciousness and transpersonal psychology in the world today'.

Wilber studied at Duke University and later at graduate school in Nebraska, pursuing degrees in chemistry and biology. However, he was also extremely interested in psychotherapy, philosophy and religion. Eventually he began to perceive a major gulf between Freudian psychology, which emphasised the strength of the ego, and the Buddhist concept of surrendering the ego in an act of transcendence. He came gradually to the view that there is a hierarchy, or spectrum of consciousness, with each part of the spectrum apparently 'real' on its own level. For Wilber the different levels were rather like boxes within larger boxes, each potentially more all-encompassing than the others. 'Just as Newtonian physics is a subset of Einsteinian physics', he maintains, 'so existentialism is a smaller Chinese box – correct as far as it goes – which is encompassed by the larger box of the transcendentalists.'[16]

Wilber himself has been substantially influenced by Theosophy, Krishnamurti and such figures as Philip Kapleau, Eido Roshi and Da Free John. His own meditative practices derive from the *Vajrayana* Tibetan Buddhist tradition which consists of oral instructions and secret teachings intended to develop wisdom and compassion, and his principal teachers have been Kalu Rinpoche and Trungpa Rinpoche. However, Wilber's spectrum model derives not so much from his meditative experience as from his remarkably far-ranging scholarly review of the 'Perennial Philosophy' encompassing the world's mystical literature, both East and West. According to Wilber,

> Human personality is a multi-levelled manifestation or expression of a single Consciousness, just as in physics the electro-magnetic spectrum is viewed as a multi-banded expression of a single, characteristic electro-magnetic wave... each level of the Spectrum is marked by a different and easily recognised sense of individual identity, which ranges from the Supreme Identity of cosmic consciousness through several gradations or bands to the drastically narrowed sense of identity associated with egoic consciousness.[17]

Wilber believes that 'man's "innermost" consciousness is identical to the absolute and ultimate reality of the universe known variously as Brahman, Tao, Dharmakaya, Allah, the Godhead – to name but a few'. He refers to these collectively as 'Mind' for, according to the Perennial Philosophy, this is all that exists in the ultimate sense. However, a problem arises because man usually operates in a dualistic state of consciousness, characterised, for example, by the distinction between 'subject' and 'object', and he thereby loses sight of this overriding One-ness. As Wilber has noted in his book *The Spectrum of Consciousness*, dualism gives rise to psychological boundaries which are perceived as real. 'We divide reality,' he writes, 'forget that we have divided it, and then forget that we have forgotten it.'[18] So each level of mind below the level of Unity Consciousness represents a progressive distortion of Mind's truly unified reality. These levels of consciousness (or illusion) represent the different states of perception which man must pass through in his quest for self-knowledge.

According to Wilber's model, the levels below the state of Unity Consciousness are like bands in a spectrum. They include the

'Transpersonal Bands' which contain the archetypes, and, below that, the Existential level which focuses on the 'total psychophysical organism as it exists in space and time'. Here cultural patterning clearly affects human perception by filtering 'reality' through language, logic and other social 'glosses'. At a lower level still, man functions not so much within a cultural matrix as within his own body-consciousness: he identifies primarily with his Ego or self-image (Intellect is assigned by the Buddhists to this level). Still lower, says Wilber, is the 'Shadow' level of existence, where man alienates part of his psyche and identifies, with an inaccurate or incomplete self-image, the Persona. The painful components of the psyche are repressed as 'evil' or undesirable.

Wilber maintains that each part of the Spectrum of Consciousness is 'marked by a different mode of knowing'. However, ultimately only Mind exists. The levels on the spectrum therefore represent different types of illusion, or *maya*, characterised by duality.

Wilber recognises that the Western psychotherapies have addressed different aspects of the Spectrum of Consciousness. For example, simple counselling and supportive therapy work at the Persona level, while psychoanalysis, psychodrama, Transactional Analysis and Reality Therapy work primarily on the Ego level. Fritz Perls' emphasis in Gestalt Therapy on recognising all aspects of the total organism, on the other hand, is very much a part of the Existential level, as Wilber sees it, and so too are Humanistic Psychology, the various encounter therapies, bioenergetics and sensory awareness. The Transpersonal level, meanwhile, is addressed in the East by Vedanta, Taoism and the *Mahayana* and *Vajrayana* forms of Buddhism and in the West by esoteric Christianity and the approaches of Maslow and Jung. As Jung has noted, 'Mystics are people who have a particularly vivid experience of the processes of the collective unconscious. Mystical experience is *experience of archetypes*.'[19]

In the Transpersonal domain the sense of dualism is suspended – one has the sense of witnessing a miraculous, mythic reality. However Wilber is still inclined to see here a subtle type of dualism, the mystic is still *witnessing* something beyond himself. 'It is when this last trace of dualism is finally and completely shattered', says Wilber, 'that one awakens to Mind, for at that moment (which is *this* moment) the witness and the witnessed are one and the same.'[20]

Wilber has been criticised for presenting a model which is hierarchical although he maintains that he has come to this view on the basis of the evidence, not by imposing his beliefs. 'The notion of hierarchy', he told Catherine Ingram during an interview for *Yoga Journal*, 'is my conclusion, not my judgement. That is, I don't particularly care whether the world is hierarchical or not. It just turns out that, if you examine all the evidence as impartially as you can, it definitely looks like some very important aspects of reality are hierarchically arranged.'

However he also pointed out that he was not saying that reality itself was hierarchical, only that the levels leading to it were:

> Absolute spirit or reality is not hierarchical. It's not qualifiable at all – it's *shunyata* or *nirguna* – unqualifiable, vast, open emptiness, without a trace of specific characteristics at all. But it manifests itself in steps, in layers, or sheaths, or grades, or levels, or whatever you want to call them, and that's hierarchy.[21]

On his own admission, Wilber does not speak as a fully realised mystic but as a student of the Perennial Philosophy, intent on presenting a workable and authentic model of consciousness. A regular meditator himself, he estimates he is presently 'at chakra one and a half, and. . .trying to work my way up to the Oedipal complex'. However, he believes his *Vajrayana* training 'seems to be accelerating this process considerably.'[22]

Even so, his Spectrum of Consciousness framework, presented in detail in such works as *The Atman Project* and *Up From Eden*, has been widely acclaimed and remains a dominant perspective in contemporary Transpersonal thought. Claire Myers Owens has described his work as 'a brilliant integration of the psychologies of East and West' and John White, himself a prolific author in these areas, has called him, quite simply, 'the long sought Einstein of consciousness research'.

Quite apart from Ken Wilber's Spectrum of Consciousness, which must necessarily remain abstract for most of us until we can confirm it as part of our life's experience, a different impulse also characterises the New Consciousness in the 1980s and that is the rising interest in Sacred Psychology and the Feminine mythic principle in particular.

Acknowledgement of the Feminine takes many different forms. It may be expressed through the sacred metaphor of Gaia – embodiment of the living planet and of the increasing global environmental awareness – or it may be through the 'Jungian' perception that a male-dominated society should learn to acquire the gifts of nurturing and intuition. And it is mirrored, too, in the revival of interest in the esoteric Wiccan and Neopagan traditions which honour the Universal Goddess through different ritual expressions. Such directions in our society are hardly surprising. As the international feminist movement helped rectify an imbalance in the socio-political sphere during the 1960s and 1970s it was surely only a matter of time before such expressions flowed through into different forms of feminine spirituality.

Margot Adler, grand-daughter of Alfred Adler, embodies this principle perfectly. A reporter for National Public Radio in New York, and the acclaimed author of *Drawing Down the Moon*, Adler says that she first fell in love with the Greek gods and goddesses when she was 12 years of age. Now an initiated Wiccan and spokesperson for the Neopagan movement in the United States she feels strongly that the esoteric and mystical traditions provide the opportunity for direct spiritual experience.

In an interview published in *East West* in October 1984 she told journalist Victoria Williams that Wicca involved 'seeing the earth as sacred, seeing human beings and everything else as part of that creation, seeing divinity as immanent and not transcendent, and seeing people as basically good'. She told me much the same thing when I interviewed her in New York for a television documentary:

> I think that one of the reasons that so many people in the United States have come to paganism is that they see in it a way of re-sacralising the world, of making it animated, of making it vivid again, of having a relationship to it that allows for harmony and wholeness. Perhaps this can help create a world that is more harmonious with Nature and can end the despoilation of the planet.[23]

However she also indicated that one of the areas where Wicca differed from more organised religions was in emphasising that the divine principle could be found, potentially, within every living person, a formal structure or belief system was not required. 'The fundamental thing about the magical and pagan religions', said Margot Adler, 'is that ultimately they say: Within yourself *you* are the god, *you* are the goddess – you can actualise within yourself and create whatever you need on this earth and beyond.'[24]

Also a key figure in the Wiccan movement is Miriam Simos, otherwise known as Starhawk, a San Francisco-based writer, counsellor and political activist. Author of *The Spiral Dance* and *Dreaming the Dark*, Starhawk studied feminism at UCLA. She regards her magical craft as the ability to transform consciousness at will and believes the female practitioner has a special and privileged role. As a representative of the Goddess, the female Wiccan is, metaphorically, a giver of life:

> The images of the Goddess as birth-giver, weaver, earth and growing plant, wind and ocean, flame, web, moon, and milk, all speak to me of connectedness, sustenance, healing, creating.
>
> If you think of magic as an art, art implies imagery and vision. The basic principle of magic is that you work with visualisation, making pictures in your mind through which you direct energy. Ritual is simply a patterned movement of energy that opens the channels to the marvellous living force we are all part of. Magical systems are highly elaborate metaphors, and through them we can identify ourselves and connect with larger forces. If magic is the art of causing change in accordance with will, then political acts, acts that speak truth to power, that push for change, are acts of magic. My model of power says that the world itself is sacred and the Goddess is simply our name for the living organism of which we're all a part.[25]

This type of mythic perception, however, extends well beyond the occult traditions of Wicca and 'Women's Mysteries'. Two other advocates of mythic renewal, Dr Jean Shinoda Bolen and Dr Jean Houston, have both come to a similar position from quite different initial perspectives.

Dr Bolen is a Jungian psychiatrist and author of such works as *Goddesses in Everywoman, Gods in Everyman* and *The Tao of Psychology*. For many years she has been advocating that each of us can apply the archetypal energies of the gods and goddesses in our lives.

Bolen trained as a doctor, was strongly influenced by the women's movement in the 1960s and taught a course on the psychology of women at the University of California's San Francisco campus. She is now Clinical Professor of Psychiatry at the University of California Medical Center.

Bolen believes, like Jung, that myths are a path to the deeper levels of the mind. In a recent interview she explained:

> Myth is a form of metaphor. It's the metaphor that's truly empowering for people. It allows us to see our ordinary lives from a different perspective, to get an intuitive sense of who we are and what is important to us. . . Myths are the bridge to the collective unconscious. They tap images, symbols, feelings, possibilities and patterns – inherent, inherited human potential that we all hold in common.[26]

While, for some, myths may perhaps have an archaic, distant quality that hardly seems relevant in everyday reality, Bolen argues quite the opposite. For her, a mythic or archetypal awareness can provide a real sense of meaning in day-to-day life:

If you live from your own depths – that is, if there is an archetypal basis for what you're doing – then there's a meaningful level to it that otherwise might be missing. . . .When people 'follow their bliss' as Joseph Campbell says, their heart is absorbed in what they're doing. People who work in an involved, deep way are doing something that matters to them just to be doing it, not for the paycheck, not for someone saying to them: 'What a good job you're doing'.[27]

The Goddess – giver of life

In her own life, and despite her Japanese ancestry, Jean Shinoda Bolen has identified, like Margot Adler, with the Greek goddesses. She told interviewer Mirka Knaster that, for her, the goddesses who had most reflected in her life were Artemis, Athena and Hestia who represented the 'independent, self-sufficient qualities in women'. Artemis, Goddess of the Hunt, seemed to embody her Japanese family's frequent moves around the United States in the 1940s, to avoid being detained in an American concentration camp; Athena, Goddess of Wisdom, seemed present in her decision to train as a medical doctor; and Hestia, Goddess of the Hearth, epitomised her present love of 'comfort in solitude'.

However, as a writer and lecturer, she has also felt drawn to Hermes, as an archetype of communication, and was at pains to point out that we can_ all embody both the gods *and* goddesses in our lives, not just the archetypes of our own gender. And, most significantly, she sees such mythic attunement as opening out into greater, planetary awareness. Echoing the sentiments of both Margot Adler and Starhawk, she explains that:

> The current need is a return to earth as the source of sacred energy. I have a concept that I share with others that we're evolving into looking out for the earth and our connection with everybody on it. Women seem more attuned to it, but increasingly more men are too. I believe that the human psyche changes collectively, when enough individuals change. Basically, the point of life is to survive and evolve. To do both requires that we recognise our planetary community and be aware that we cannot do anything negative to our enemies without harming ourselves. I think that we may be evolving – but then, I'm an optimistic soul.[28]

Dr Jean Houston, also a strong advocate of archetypal psychology, takes much the same position, and is similarly attuned to the new 'Gaia consciousness'. 'The Earth is a living system', she says. 'That is why women are now being released from the exclusivity of a child-bearing, child-rearing role. This is also the time when the Earth desparately needs the ways of thinking and being that women have developed through hundreds of thousands of years.'

Jean Houston is a former president of the Association for Humanistic Psychology and director of the Foundation for Mind Research in Pomona, New York, but her talents also extend into creative spiritual expression. An award-winning actress in Off-Broadway theatre, she has developed training programmes in spiritual studies which include the enactment of themes from the ancient Mystery traditions.

She also trained as a classics scholar in ancient languages and, like Dr Stanislav Grof, has a background in psychedelic research. She co-authored *The Varieties of Psychedelic Experience* and *Psychedelic Art* in the late 1960s and her more recent books include *The Possible Human* and *The Search for the Beloved*.

Houston is especially intrigued by the role that myth can play in shaping consciousness, and for several years has been working with the themes in Sacred Psychology. Of particular interest to her are the sacred journeys of human transformation including such figures as Parsifal and the Holy Grail, St Francis, Odysseus, Christ and Isis, for all of these are examples of how we may undertake a quest of spiritual renewal.

In an article published in *Dromenon* in 1981 she explained that: 'In my work I try to teach people how to repattern and extend the uses of brain, body and symbolic knowing in order that they may become adequate vehicles for their own powerful psyches.'[29]

One of her techniques at this time was to ask participants to learn 'shape shiftings' by relaxing and identifying with different 'god-identities', thereby acquiring archetypal perceptions. Such roles might include meditating on such figures as the Great Mother, the Wise Old King, the Young Redeemer, the Trickster or the Holy Child.

But Houston now emphasises that such visualisations in themselves are not enough. It may well be that some sense of personal conflict is required to spur one on in the spiritual quest. Personal growth, she feels, can grow from the sense of being 'wounded', expressed, perhaps, in the feeling of being abandoned or hurt in some way. 'God', she says, 'may reach us through our affliction . . . we can be ennobled and extended by looking at this wounding in such a way that we move from the personal particular to the personal universal.'[30]

She expanded on these ideas in a recent interview in *Magical Blend*:

> So much of my work is. . .essentially a form of Sacred Theatre. I take the great stories, like Psyche and Eros, or Oedipus, or Faust, any of the stories of the Hero with a Thousand Faces or the Heroine, Demeter and Persephone, the Gnostic Sophia. . .. There's something about the Great Story or the Great Myth that moves you beyond your personal particularity into the personal universal. Suddenly, you have not just brought a context and larger capacities; you literally *take on* the eyes of Athena, the taste buds of Dionysus, the yearning of Odysseus for home,

the passion of Parsifal for the Grail. These large emotions are evoked in you because you are really part of a Larger Story, just as we are part of the air we breathe and the environment that we are in.[31]

Houston also likes very much to work in groups for she has found, experientially, that this helps to awaken in each person the sense of participating in a mythic reality:

We need the symbiosis with others. That's why I like to work in groups. . . .. There's more to share, more images. There are more aspects and alternatives, so more can happen. Group energy helps us grow. . .

The Story is larger than you and the group, so you can find a relatively open space within it to discover what in the Story speaks directly to you and your unique life experience. The Story frees us.[32]

THE JOURNEY OF HUMAN POTENTIAL

The essential message which emerges from thinkers like Jean Shinoda Bolen and Jean Houston – and also earlier pioneers of archetypal consciousness like Carl Jung – is that we should all endeavour to learn ways of tapping the sacred potential which is latent within our being. Various forms of ritual, theatre, ceremonial, meditation and visualisation can all assist this process but, at heart, the task for each of us is to rediscover the spiritual and universal in the everyday experience. This then becomes very much a personal quest, our own individual journey of the spirit. During our lifetime this may lead us along many different paths and through the company of many other guides and teachers, until we glimpse a perspective that is real for us: a situation in which the universal, as Jean Houston says, becomes particular to our own experience.

However, it seems to me quite crucial that if the process is to be a journey of self-discovery, each of us should endeavour to awaken our spiritual potential in the most instinctual ways we can find, allowing the sacred to rise up from within our inner depths rather than submerging ourselves in imposed belief systems. There is an implicit message here also for devotees of institutionalised or doctrinaire forms of religious belief and also new religious groupings headed by dominant spiritual leaders. The questions we should all ask are: 'Does my adopted framework, my present 'spiritual path', allow me to grow in my perspectives? Does it open me to ever larger, more transcendent realms of spiritual experience? Or am I being limited by my present belief system and thereby, consciously or unconsciously, imposing barriers which define an enclosed and secure 'spiritual reality' I feel safe with?' In the final analysis there is no-one who can supply these answers but ourselves.

A book like this really has no ending or formal conclusion. I feel we are living in exciting times – times of enormous social change, of interwoven communications networks and rapidly developing technology. But underlying the Human Potential Movement and the New Age alike is a call that we should increasingly trust our own intuitions, our own perceptions, our own core sense of meaning. For rapid social change can be seen either as a threat or a challenge. It can lead us to cling desparately to the old ways of doing things which have perhaps outlived their usefulness, or it can open us to new types of connectedness, new bonds with others, new frontiers of learning, new global awareness.

It does not surprise me at all that we should also be seeing, in the present time, a resurgence of fundamentalist Islam and fundamentalist Christianity – for these forms of religious expression represent an earnest attachment to rigid belief systems which define fixed boundaries and categories like 'good' and 'evil'; 'follower' and 'infidel'; 'orthodox' and 'heretical'; 'worshipper' and 'blasphemer'. Little surprise, then, that for many devotees of such traditions, the issues posed by the Human Potential Movement and the very idea of 'personal growth' are deeply unsettling. Here we have an emerging perspective which in the ultimate sense poses no security at all, for if Ken Wilber's Spectrum of Consciousness, Mahayana Buddhism and the mystical Jewish Kabbalah are in any sense correct, our most familiar sense of 'self', the ego we all identify with, must in due course open out into an infinite Void of Spirit.

So who can say, in this sense, where the journey of transformation will take us, or whether we will ever 'arrive' at a place like 'Heaven' or 'enlightenment'? The evidence of the Human Potential Movement, of psychedelic research, and of the New Physics, is telling us that the most complete picture we now have of the Universe is one of flux, of change, of interconnectedness – all in turn flowing from an essential One-ness.

At the most profound levels of consciousness the boundaries melt, the barriers fall away, the particular becomes universal. So, the journey which leads us towards realising our own potential can be nothing more, or less, than a journey which takes us towards the infinite essence of our own Being.

NOTES

1. BRAIN, MIND AND CONSCIOUSNESS

1. J.B. Watson, 'Psychology as the behaviourist views it', *Psychological Review*, 20:158–1977, 1913.
2. B.F. Skinner, *About Behaviorism*, Knopf, 1974, p. 225.
3. See Paul D. Maclean, 'The Paranoid Streak in Man' in *Beyond Reductionism* by Arthur Koestler and J.R. Smythies (eds.), Beacon Press, 1969; and C. Hampden-Turner, *Maps of the Mind*, Mitchell Beazley, 1981, pp. 80–3.
4. R. Ornstein, *The Psychology of Consciousness*, Cape, 1975, p. 64.
5. David Galin, 'The Two Modes of Consciousness and the Two Halves of the Brain' in P.R. Lee et al. *Symposium on Consciousness*, 1977, p. 40.
6. R. Ornstein, *Multimind*, Macmillan, 1986, pp. 35–6.
7. Ibid., p. 43.
8. Ibid., p. 81.
9. R. Ornstein, *The Psychology of Consciousness*, p. 17.
10. Karl Pribram, 'The Holographic Hypothesis of Brain Functioning' in S. Grof (ed.), *Ancient Wisdom, Modern Science*, pp. 174–5.
11. Ibid., p. 178.
12. Karl Pribram, 'Behaviorism, Phenomenology and Holism' in Valle & von Eckartsberg, (eds), *The Metaphors of Consciousness*, p. 148.
13. Karl Pribram in Grof, op. cit., pp. 178–9.

2. PIONEERS OF HUMAN POTENTIAL

1. William James, *Psychology: the Briefer Course*, Holt, 1892, p. 1.
2. William James, *The Varieties of Religious Experience*, New American Library, 1958, p. 298.
3. Quoted in Gardner Murphy and Robert Ballou (eds.), *William James on Psychical Research*, Viking, 1960, p. 324.
4. William James, *The Will to Believe and Other Essays in Popular Philosophy*, Longmans, Green & Co, p. 232.
5. William James, *The Principles of Psychology*, vol. 2, Dover, 1950, p. 560 (first published 1890).
6. William James, *Talks to Teachers on Psychology and to Students on Some of Life's Ideals*, Holt, 1899; Dover, 1962, p. 100.
7. J. Fadiman and R. Frager, *Personality and Personal Growth*, Harper & Row, 1976, p. 201.
8. William James, *The Varieties of Religious Experience*, p. 391.

9. Ilham Dilman, *Freud and the Mind*, Basil Blackwell, 1986, p. 7.
10. J. Fadiman and R. Frager, *Personality and Personal Growth*, p. 14
11. Gardner Murphy, *An Historical Introduction to Modern Psychology*, Routledge & Kegan Paul, 1967.
12. S. Freud, *New Introductory Lectures on Psychoanalysis*, vol. 22, Norton, 1949, p. 80.
13. J. Fadiman and R. Frager, *Personality and Personal Growth*, p. 20.
14. I. Dilman, *Freud and the Mind*, p. 125.
15. See Frank J. Sulloway, *Freud: Biologist of the Mind*, Basic Books, p. 338.
16. S. Freud, *The Interpretation of Dreams*, standard edition, vols. 4–5, quoted in J. Fadiman and R. Frager, op. cit., p. 21.
17. C.G. Jung, *Memories, Dreams, Reflections*, Random House, 1961, pp. 168–9.
18. C.G. Jung *Man and his Symbols*, Dell, 1968, p. 13.
19. Ibid., p. 18.
20. Ibid., pp. 41–2.
21. C.G. Jung, *Two Essays in Analytical Psychology*, Routledge & Kegan Paul, 1953, p. 68.
22. Ibid., pp. 65–6.
23. Ibid., p. 70.
24. C.G. Jung, 'The Relations Between the Ego and the Unconscious', in *Collected Works*, 1928, p. 176.
25. H.L. Ansbacher and R. Ansbacher (eds.) *The Individual Psychology of Alfred Adler: a systematic presentation in selections from his writings*, Harper, 1956, p. 104.
26. See J. Fadiman and R. Frager, *Personality and Personal Growth*, p. 97.
27. Quoted in H.L. Ansbacher and R. Ansbacher, *The Individual Psychology of Alfred Adler*, p. 177.
28. J. Fadiman and R. Frager, *Personality and Personal Growth*, p. 99.
29. H.L. Ansbacher and R. Ansbacher (eds.) *Alfred Adler: Superiority and Social Interest, a Collection of Later Writings*, Viking, 1964, p. 69.

3. TOWARDS THE TRANSPERSONAL

1. Abraham Maslow, *Motivation and Personality*, Harper & Row, 1970, p. 150.
2. Abraham Maslow, *The Farther Reaches of Human Nature*, Viking, 1971, p. 47.
3. Quoted in Anthony J. Sutich, 'The Emergence of the Transpersonal Orientation: A Personal Account', *Journal of Transpersonal Psychology*, 1976, vol. 8, no. 1, p. 6.
4. Anthony J. Sutich, 'The Founding of Humanistic and Transpersonal Psychology: A Personal Account', dissertation presented to the Humanistic Psychology Institute, April 1976, p. 22.
5. Ibid., p. 23.
6. Ibid., p. 29.
7. Ibid., p. 35.
8. Ibid., p. 45.

9. Ibid., pp. 59–60.
10. Ibid., p. 114.
11. Ibid., p. 115.
12. Ibid., p. 148.
13. Ibid., p. 150.
14. Ibid., p. 155.
15. Ibid., p. 167.
16. Ibid., p. 172.

4. ESALEN, GESTALT AND ENCOUNTER

1. Frederik S. Perls, *In and Out of the Garbage Pail*, The Real People Press, 1969, p. 115.
2. Quoted in *Fritz* by Martin Shepard, Saturday Review Press/E.P. Dutton, 1975 pp. 8–9.
3. Frederick S. Perls, *In and Out of the Garbage Pail*, p. 272.
4. Quoted in M. Shephard, *Fritz*, p. 214.
5. Frederick S. Perls, *Gestalt Therapy Verbatim*, The Real People Press, 1969, p. 4.
6. Ibid., p. 68.
7. William Schutz, *Joy: Expanding Human Awareness*, Grove Press, 1967, p. 15.

5. THE PSYCHEDELIC YEARS

1. Quoted in Gene Anthony, *The Summer of Love: Haight–Ashbury at its Highest*, Celestial Arts, 1980, p. 29.
2. Joe David Brown (ed.) *The Hippies*, Time-Life Books, 1967, pp. 39–40.
3. Quoted in G. Anthony, *The Summer of Love*, p. 129.
4. Ibid., p. 155.
5. Ibid., p. 156.
6. Timothy Leary, *Flashbacks*, J.P. Tarcher, 1983, p. 29.
7. Timothy Leary, *High Priest*, 1968, p. 25.
8. Timothy Leary, *The Politics of Ecstasy*, 1970, p. 112.
9. Ibid., p. 131.
10. Ibid., p. 15.
11. W.Y. Evans–Wentz (ed.) *The Tibetan Book of the Dead*, 1960.

6. MAPS FOR INNER SPACE

1. Ralph Metzner, *Maps of Consciousness*, 1971, p. 9.
2. Heinrich Zimmer, *The King and the Corpse*, Meridian Books, 1960, p. 178.
3. For further details on the archetypal content of the Major Arcana in the Tarot see N. Drury, *Inner Visions: Explorations in Magical Consciousness*, 1979 (chapter three).
4. For additional background information see John Lilly, *The Centre of the Cyclone*, Calder & Boyars, 1973, and *The Human Biocomputer*, Abacus, 1974.

5. Interview with the author during filming for *The Occult Experience* television documentary, Esalen Institute, December 1984.
6. S. Grof and J. Halifax, *The Human Encounter with Death*, 1979, pp. 47–8.
7. Ibid., p. 51.
8. S. Grof, 'Modern Consciousness Research and the Quest for a New Paradigm', *Re-Vision*, vol 2, no 1, Winter/Spring 1979, pp. 42–3.
9. Interview with the author, Esalen Institute, 1984.
10. S. Grof, 'Modern Consciousness Research', p. 44.

7. THE HOLISTIC PERSPECTIVE

1. Interview with the author, Esalen Institute, 1984.
2. Syed Abdullah, 'Meditation: Achieving Internal Balance', in Elliot M. Goldwag (ed.) *Inner Balance: The Power of Holistic Healing*, p. 109.
3. S. Miller et al. *Dimensions of Humanistic Medicine*, Institute for the Study of Humanistic Medicine, 1975.
4. By contrast, the Type B person was much calmer, had more inner composure and was less demonstrative in his actions. He could be as equally self-motivated as Type A, but his behaviour was not as overtly competitive or aggressive.
5. Carl and Stephanie Simonton, 'The Role of the Mind in Cancer Therapy' in R.J. Carlson (ed.) *The Frontiers of Medicine*, 1976.
6. R. Wechsler, 'A New Prescription: Mind Over Malady', *Discover*, February 1987, p. 59.

8. THE 'NEW AGE' AND BEYOND

1. Deborah Cameron, 'Satan and the Showgirl: The New Age under Fire' in *Good Weekend*, 11 March 1989, p. 20.
2. Ibid.
3. Reported in *New Age News*, vol. 1, no. 10, December 1987, p. 1.
4. Quoted in Ellic Howe, *The Magicians of the Golden Dawn*, 1972, p. 127.
5. Included in the press-kit for Sri Chinmoy's tour of Australia and New Zealand, November–December 1987.
6. Ibid.
7. Ibid.
8. Workshops held in Sydney in February 1985 – advertisement personally endorsed by Elizabeth Clare Prophet.
9. 'Ma Anand Sheela Interview on Cable News Network', *The Rajneesh Times*, vol. 3, no. 5, 9 August 1985, p. A4.
10. Catherine Ingram, 'Ken Wilber: The Pundit of Transpersonal Psychology' in *Yoga Journal*, September/October 1987, p. 49.
11. Quoted in W.W. Bartley, *Werner Erhard*, Clarkson Potter, 1978, p. 74.
12. Reprinted in *New Age News*, vol. 2, no. 1, April 1988.
13. Ibid.

14. Personal interview with Alexander Everett, Sydney, November 1988, and extract from interview in *Life Quest*, May/June 1988.
15. Personal interview with Alexander Everett, Sydney, November 1988.
16. Catherine Ingram, 'Ken Wilber: The Pundit of Transpersonal Psychology', p. 40.
17. Ken Wilber, 'Psychologia Perennis: The Spectrum of Consciousness' in Roger N. Walsh and Frances Vaughan (ed.) *Beyond Ego*, J.P. Tarcher, 1980, pp. 74–5.
18. Ken Wilber, The Spectrum of Consciousness, Quest Books, 1977, p. 241.
19. C.G. Jung, *Analytical Psychology: Its Theory and Practice*, Vintage Books, 1968, p. 110.
20. Ken Wilber, 'Psychologia Perennis: The Spectrum of Consciousness', p. 83.
21. Catherine Ingram, 'Ken Wilber: The Pundit of Transpersonal Psychology', p. 44.
22. Ibid., p. 47.
23. Quoted in N. Drury, *The Occult Experience*, Fontana/Collins, 1985, p. 44 (Hale, 1987; Avery, 1989).
24. Ibid.
25. Quoted in Victoria Williams, 'The Sacred Craft', *East West*, October 1984.
26. Mirka Knaster, 'The Goddesses in Jean Shinoda Bolen', *East West*, March 1989, p. 45.
27. Ibid., p. 44.
28. Ibid., p. 73.
29. Jean Houston, 'Myth and Pathos in Sacred Psychology', *Dromenon*, vol. 3, no. 2, Spring 1981, p. 32.
30. Ibid., p. 33.
31. Richard Daab, 'An Interview with Jean Houston' (Part One), *Magical Blend*, no. 18, February–April 1988, p. 25.
32. Ibid. (Part Three), *Magical Blend*, no. 20, August–October 1988, pp. 23–4.

Bibliography

Abdullah, S. 'Meditation: Achieving Internal Balance' in E. Goldwag (ed.) *Inner Balance*, Prentice-Hall, 1979.

Achterberg, J. *Imagery in Healing*, Shambhala, 1985.

Adler, M. *Drawing Down the Moon*, Beacon Press, 1988.

Anderson, W.T. *The Upstart Spring: Esalen and the American Awakening*, Addison–Wesley, 1983.

Ansbacher H.L. & Ansbacher, R. *The Individual Psychology of Alfred Adler: a systematic presentation in selections from his writings*, Harper, 1956.

—*Alfred Adler: Superiority and Social Interest – A Collection of Later Writings*, Viking, 1964.

Anthony, G. *The Summer of Love: Haight–Ashbury at its Highest*, Celestial Arts, 1980.

Assagioli, R. *Psychosynthesis*, Viking, 1971.

Bartley, W.W. *Werner Erhard*, Clarkson Potter, 1978.

Bliss, S. (ed.) *The New Holistic Health Workbook*, Stephen Greene Press/Viking-Penguin, 1985.

Boadella, D. *Wilhelm Reich: The Evolution of his Work*, Arkana, 1985.

Bohm, D. *Wholeness and the Implicate Order*, Routledge & Kegan Paul, 1980.

—*The Tao of Psychology*, Harper & Row, 1979.

Bolen, J.S. *Goddesses in Everywoman*, Harper & Row, 1985.

—*Gods in Everyman*, Harper & Row, 1989.

Brown, J.D. *The Hippies* Time-Life Books, 1967.

Cade, M. and Coxhead, N. *The Awakened Mind*, Wildwood House, 1979.

Cameron, D. 'Satan and the Showgirl: The New Age Under Fire' in *Good Weekend*, 11 March 1989.

Campbell, J. *The Hero with a Thousand Faces*, Pantheon, 1949.

Capra, F. *The Tao of Physics*, Shambhala, 1975.

Carlson, R.J. (ed.) *The Frontiers of Science and Medicine*, Regnery, 1975.

Daab, R. 'An Interview with Jean Houston', Berkeley, *Magical Blend* issues 18, 19 and 20, 1988.

Dilman, I. *Freud and the Mind*, Basil Blackwell, 1986.

Drury, N. *Inner Visions: Explorations in Magical Consciousness*, Routledge & Kegan Paul, 1979.

—*The Healing Power*, Muller, 1981.

—*The Bodywork Book*, Prism Press, 1984.

—*Don Juan, Mescalito and Modern Magic*, Arkana, 1985.

—*Inner Health*, Prism Press, 1985.

—*The Occult Experience*, Avery, 1989.

—*Shamanism*, Element, 1989.

Edinger, E. *Ego and Archetype*, Penguin, 1973.

THE ELEMENTS OF HUMAN POTENTIAL

Evans-Wentz, W.Y. (ed.) *The Tibetan Book of the Dead*, Oxford University Press, 1960.

Everett, A. Interview with Alexander Everett, *Nature & Health*, September 1989.

Fadiman, J. & Frager, R. *Personality and Personal Growth*, Harper & Row, 1976.

Freud, S. *New Introductory Lectures on Psychoanalysis*, Norton, 1949.

—*The Interpretation of Dreams*, Avon Books, 1967.

Galin, D. 'The Two Modes of Consciousness and the Two Halves of the Brain' in P.R. Lee (ed.) *Symposium on Consciousness*, Penguin, 1977.

Gawain, S. *Creative Visualization*, Whatever Publishing, 1978.

—*Living in the Light*, Whatever Publishing, 1981.

Gawler, I. *Peace of Mind*, Prism Press, 1989.

Goldwag, E. (ed.) *Inner Balance*, Prentice-Hall, 1979.

Goleman, D. (ed.) *Consciousness: Brain, States of Awareness and Mysticism*, Harper & Row, 1979.

—*The Meditative Mind*, Tarcher, 1988.

Green, E. & Green, A. *Beyond Biofeedback*, Delacorte, 1977.

Grof, S. *Realms of the Human Unconscious*, Dutton, 1976.

—'Modern Consciousness Research and the Quest for a New Paradigm', *Re-Vision*, vol. 2, no. 1, Winter/Spring 1979.

—*LSD Psychotherapy*, Hunter House, 1980.

—*Ancient Wisdom, Modern Science*, State University of New York Press, 1984.

—*Beyond the Brain*, State University of New York Press, 1985.

—*The Adventure of Self-Discovery*, State University of New York Press, 1988.

Grof. S. & Halifax, J. *The Human Encounter with Death*, Dutton, 1979.

Hagon, Z. *Channelling: The Spiritual Connection*, Prism Press, 1989.

Hampden-Turner, C. *Maps of the Mind*, Mitchell Beazley, 1981.

Harner, M. *The Way of the Shaman*, Harper & Row, 1980.

Houston, J. 'Myth and Pathos in Sacred Psychology', *Dromenon*, vol. 3, no. 2, Spring 1981.

—*The Possible Human*, Tarcher, 1986.

—*The Search for the Beloved*, Tarcher, 1987.

Howe, E. *The Magicians of the Golden Dawn*, Routledge & Kegan Paul, 1972.

Huxley, A. *The Perennial Philosophy*, Chatto & Windus, 1946.

—*The Doors of Perception/Heaven & Hell*, Penguin, 1963.

—*Moksha: Writings on Psychedelics and the Visionary Experience*, Stonehill, 1977.

Ingram, C. 'Ken Wilber: The Pundit of Transpersonal Psychology', *Yoga Journal*, September/October 1987.

James, W. *Psychology: The Briefer Course*, Holt, 1892.

—*The Will to Believe and Other Essays in Popular Philosophy*, Longmans Green & Co, 1902.

—*The Varieties of Religious Experience*, New American Library, 1958.

—*Talks to Teachers on Psychology and to Students on Some of Life's Ideals*, Dover, 1962.

Jung, C.G. *Two Essays in Analytical Psychology*, Routledge & Kegan Paul, 1953.
—*Symbols of Transformation*, Bollingen Foundation, 1956.
—*Memories, Dreams, Reflections*, Random House, 1961.
—*Analytical Psychology: its Theory and Practice*, Vintage Books, 1968.
—*Man and his Symbols*, Dell, 1968.
Kamiya, J. *Biofeedback and Self-Control: A Reader*, Aldine, 1971.
Kaplan, A. *Meditation and Kabbalah*, Weiser, 1982.
Knaster, M. 'The Goddesses in Jean Shinnoda Bolen', *East West*, March 1989.
Knight, J.Z. *A State of Mind*, Warner Books, 1987.
Koestler, A. & Smythies, J.R. *Beyond Reductionism*, Beacon Press, 1969.
Leary, T. *The Psychedelic Experience*, University Books, 1964.
—*High Priest*, New American Library, 1968.
—*The Politics of Ecstasy*, Paladin, 1970.
—*Flashbacks*, Tarcher, 1983.
Le Shan, L. *The Medium, the Mystic and the Physicist*, Viking, 1974.
Lee, P.R. (ed.) *Symposium on Consciousness*, Penguin, 1971.
Lilly, J. *The Centre of the Cyclone*, Calder and Boyars, 1973.
—*The Human Biocomputer*, Abacus, 1974.
—*Simulations of God*, Simon and Schuster, 1976.
—*The Deep Self: Profound Relaxation and the Tank Isolation Technique*, Simon and Schuster, 1977.
Luton, L. 'Reichian and Neo-Reichian Therapy' in N. Drury (ed.) *The Bodywork Book*, Prism Press, 1984.
Maclean, P.D. 'The Paranoid Streak in Man' in A. Koestler and J.R. Smythies (eds.), *Beyond Reductionism*, Beacon Press, 1969.
Maltz, M. *Psycho-Cybernetics*, Pocket Books, 1966.
Maslow, A. *Motivation and Personality*, Harper & Row, 1970.
—*The Farther Reaches of Human Nature*, Viking, 1971.
Masters, R. & Houston, J. *The Varieties of Psychedelic Experience*, Holt Rinehart and Winston, 1966.
—*Psychedelic Art* Grove Press, 1968.
—*Mind Games*, Turnstone Books, 1973.
Meares, A, *Cancer – Another Way?* Hill of Content, 1980.
—*The Wealth Within*, Hill of Content, 1981.
—*A Way of Doctoring*, Hill of Content, 1984.
Metzner, R. *The Ecstatic Adventure*, Macmillan, 1968.
—*Maps of Consciousness*, Collier-Macmillan, 1971.
—*Opening to Inner Light*, Century, 1987.
Miller, S. *Dimensions of Humanistic Medicine*, Institute for the Study of Humanistic Medicine, 1975.
Murphy, G. *An Historical Introduction to Modern Psychology*, Routledge & Kegan Paul, 1967.
Murphy, G. & Ballou, R. *William James on Psychical Research*, Viking, 1960.
Ornstein, R. *The Psychology of Consciousness*, Cape, 1975.
—*Multimind*, Macmillan, 1986.
Orr, L. *Rebirthing in the New Age*, Celestial Arts, 1980.
Pelletier, K. *Holistic Medicine*, Delta Books, 1979.

Perls, F.S. *Gestalt Therapy Verbatim*, Real People Press, 1969.

—*In and Out of the Garbage Pail*, Real People Press, 1969.

Ponce, C. *Kabbalah*, Garnstone Press, 1974.

Pribram, K. *Languages of the Brain*, Prentice Hall, 1971.

—'Behaviorism, Phenomenology and Holism in Psychology: A Scientific Analysis' in R.S. Valle and R. von Eckartsberg, *The Metaphors of Consciousness*, Plenum Press, 1981.

—'The Holographic Hypothesis of Brain Functioning' in S. Grof (ed.) *Ancient Wisdom, Modern Science*, State University of New York Press, 1984.

Rajneesh, S. *The Rajneesh Bible* (vols. 1 and 2), Rajneesh Foundation International, 1985.

Ram Dass *Doing Your Own Being*, Spearman, 1973.

—*The Only Dance There Is*, Doubleday, 1974.

—*Journey of Awakening*, Doubleday, 1978.

—*Grist for the Mill*, Bantam, 1979.

Rogers, C. *Carl Rogers on Encounter Groups*, Harper & Row, 1970.

Sagan, C. *The Dragons of Eden*, Random House, 1977.

Samuels, M. & Samuels, N. *Seeing with the Mind's Eye*, Random House/-Bookworks, 1975.

Schutz, W. *Joy: Expanding Human Awareness*, Grove Press, 1967.

—*Here Comes Everybody*, Harper & Row, 1971.

Selye, H. *Stress Without Distress*, Dutton, 1974.

Shepard, M. *Fritz*, Dutton/Saturday Review Press, 1975.

Simonton, C. & Simonton, S. 'The Role of the Mind in Cancer Therapy' in R.J. Carlson (ed.), *The Frontiers of Medicine*, Regnery, 1976.

—*Getting Well Again*, Tarcher, 1978.

Skinner, B.F. *About Behaviorism*, Knopf, 1974.

Stace, W.T. *Mysticism and Philosophy*, Macmillan, 1960.

—*The Teachings of the Mystics*, New American Library, 1960.

Starhawk *The Spiral Dance*, Harper & Row, 1979.

—*Dreaming the Dark*, Beacon Press, 1982.

Stevens, J. *Storming Heaven: LSD and the American Dream*, Atlantic Monthly Press, 1987.

Sulloway, F.J. *Freud: Biologist of the Mind*, Basic Books, 1979.

Sutich, A.J. 'The Emergence of the Transpersonal Orientation: a Personal Account', *Journal of Transpersonal Psychology*, vol. 8, no. 1, 1976.

—'The Founding of Humanistic and Transpersonal Psychology', Humanistic Psychology Institute, degree dissertation, April 1976.

Tart, C. (ed.) *Altered States of Consciousness*, Wiley, 1969.

—*Transpersonal Psychologies*, Harper & Row, 1975.

Valle, R.S. & von Eckartsberg, R. (ed.) *The Metaphors of Consciousness*, Plenum Press, 1981.

Walsh, R.N. & Vaughan, F. (ed.) *Beyond Ego*, Tarcher, 1980.

Watson, J.B. 'Psychology as the Behaviourist Views It', *Psychological Review*, 20: 158–1977.

Watts, A. *The Joyous Cosmology*, Vintage Books, 1962.

Wechsler, R. 'A New Prescription: Mind Over Malady', *Discover*, February 1987.

White, J. (ed.) *The Highest State of Consciousness*, Doubleday Anchor, 1972.
Wilber, K. *The Spectrum of Consciousness*, Quest Books, 1977.
—*No Boundary*, Center Publications, 1979.
—*The Atman Project*, Quest Books, 1980.
—'Psychologia Perennis: The Spectrum of Consciousness' in R.N. Walsh and F. Vaughan (eds.) *Beyond Ego*, Tarcher, 1980.
—*Up From Eden*, Doubleday Anchor, 1981.
Williams, V. 'The Sacred Craft', *East West*, October 1984.
Zimmer, H. *The King and the Corpse*, Meridian, 1960.
Zukav, G. *The Dancing Wu Li Masters: An Overview of the New Physics*, Morrow, 1979.

INDEX